Genealogy
and the Law
in Canada

D0862713

GENEALOGIST'S REFERENCE SHELF

Genealogy

and the Law

in Canada

DR. MARGARET ANN WILKINSON

Withdrawn
University of Waterloo

DUNDURN PRESS
TORONTO

Copyright © Dr. Margaret Ann Wilkinson, 2010

All rights reserved. No part of this publication may be reproduced, stored in a retrieval system, or transmitted in any form or by any means, electronic, mechanical, photocopying, recording, or otherwise (except for brief passages for purposes of review) without the prior permission of Dundurn Press and the Ontario Genealogical Society. Permission to photocopy should be requested from Access Copyright.

Editor: Ruth Chernia   Proofreader: Cheryl Hawley
Design: Courtney Horner   Printer: Transcontinental

Library and Archives Canada Cataloguing in Publication

Wilkinson, Margaret Ann
Genealogy and the law in Canada / Margaret Ann Wilkinson.

(Genealogist's reference shelf)
Co-published by: Ontario Genealogical Society.
ISBN 978-1-55488-452-0

1. Genealogy--Law and legislation--Canada.   2. Freedom of information--Canada.   I. Ontario Genealogical Society II. Title. III. Series: Genealogist's reference shelf

KE4422.W54 2010   342.7108'53   C2009-907198-3
KF4774.W54 2010

1 2 3 4 5   14 13 12 11 10

Conseil des Arts du Canada   Canada Council for the Arts   Canada   ONTARIO ARTS COUNCIL CONSEIL DES ARTS DE L'ONTARIO

We acknowledge the support of the **Canada Council for the Arts** and the **Ontario Arts Council** for our publishing program. We also acknowledge the financial support of the **Government of Canada** through the **Book Publishing Industry Development Program** and **The Association for the Export of Canadian Books,** and the **Government of Ontario** through the **Ontario Book Publishers Tax Credit program,** and the **Ontario Media Development Corporation.**

This book is based upon the law in Canada as of June 2009. This book cannot substitute for legal advice. Please consult a lawyer qualified to practise in your province or territory to obtain specific legal opinions about specific situations that concern you.

Care has been taken to trace the ownership of copyright material used in this book. The author and the publisher welcome any information enabling them to rectify any references or credits in subsequent editions.

J. Kirk Howard, President

Printed and bound in Canada.
www.dundurn.com

Ontario Genealogical Society
Suite 102, 40 Orchard View Boulevard
Toronto, Ontario, Canada M4R 1B9
tel. (416) 489-0734   fax. (416) 489-9803
provoffice@ogs.on.ca   www.ogs.on.ca

Dundurn Press	Gazelle Book Services Limited	Dundurn Press
3 Church Street, Suite 500	White Cross Mills	2250 Military Road
Toronto, Ontario, Canada	High Town, Lancaster, England	Tonawanda, NY
M5E 1M2	LA1 4XS	U.S.A. 14150

CONTENTS

DEDICATION AND ACKNOWLEDGEMENTS

This book was inspired by the dedicated work in genealogy that my mother-in-law, Yvonne June (Ferguson) Crouch undertook before her untimely death, in order to provide a legacy for her three grandchildren (Nicole Amor Crouch-Diaz, Meredith Yvonne Crouch, and George Gregory Richard Crouch). Yvonne was a very active member of the Ontario Genealogical Society, Kingston Branch. My ongoing interest in genealogy is fuelled by the wonderful family archives amassed and organized by my own mother, Isobel Ellen (Althouse) Wilkinson, before her death.

The immediate impetus for the research leading to the series of articles and talks on which this book is based was an invitation to speak, facilitated by my cousin-in-law, once removed, Carolyn Croke, at The Ontario Genealogical Society in London. I would like to thank, as well, those who asked questions during the talks around the province of Ontario to which I was invited while working on this project.

I am indebted to former law student Leo Law and current law student Justin Vessair for assistance in the editing preparation of this manuscript, as well as to former law students Chad Matheson and Lovejeet Bajwa for research assistance on earlier versions of this work. I am also exceedingly grateful for the guidance, advice, and patience of my editor at the Ontario Genealogical Society, Ruth Chernia. All of this work investigating the interrelationships between intellectual property (including copyright) and privacy (and its derivative, personal data protection), as well as other aspects of information law and policy, has been funded over the years through grants received from the Social Sciences and Humanities Research Council of Canada.

INTRODUCTION

As you know, genealogy is a fascinating study. Doing genealogical research is essentially an exercise in information-gathering. This may explain why genealogists are one of the most important (if not *the* most important) users of the services and resources of public libraries in Canada today. Increasingly, however, we are told that we are in the "information age" — and one result of this new state of affairs is that information is becoming an engine of our economy. As such, information is more and more viewed from the perspective of its commercial value.

On the other hand, democracies traditionally view access to information as a cornerstone, enabling societies to remain free and democratic. The organs of the law (legislatures and the judiciary) are becoming involved in striking a balance between these two impulses. Because genealogists are intimately involved with information, a number of these changes in the legal environment have a direct impact on your work.

Since most of the population of North America reflects the immigrant experience, either in this or previous centuries, doing genealogical research, for most people, is a fascinating exercise in local, regional, national, and international information-gathering. The development of digital records and broad access to the web has revolutionized the ways in which genealogists approach their investigations — and has made it much easier to locate information relevant to any particular genealogical inquiry from sources often separated by vast distances.

The law, on the other hand, remains very connected to particular geographic locations. The legislatures and governments of any particular country can only create law that affects their own geographic territory. Strictly speaking, countries *can* claim jurisdiction over their citizens, wherever situated, but, for the purpose of the laws discussed in this book, it will be understood that the provinces, territories, and federal government in Canada have legislated with intent to affect those situated within their respective borders. Thus, in undertaking genealogical research that involves materials located beyond Canada's borders, you will have to consult other sources about the applicable laws. This book will discuss the relevant laws applicable to those working within Canada with materials that are located, at the time you are doing the work, in Canada.

In the first chapter, I discuss material located in particular organizations *in Canada*. In the second chapter, the focus is on genealogists *in Canada* who are doing genealogical investigations for pay. In the third chapter, I describe the law relating to information found in cemeteries located *in Canada*. The fourth chapter contains an exploration of Canadian copyright law, which applies to the handling, in Canada, of any materials, no matter where they were written or published or are currently housed. The fifth and final chapter is the law of libel in Canada and how it may become connected with genealogy. The fifth chapter will be helpful to any genealogist, professional or amateur, who publishes material in Canada.

Introduction

If you are reading this book and are situated *outside* Canada, the discussions in Chapters 1 and 3 may be directly relevant to your research. The discussions in Chapters 2 and 4 will not be directly relevant to your own activities but may explain the attitudes of your acquaintances located in Canada. The discussions in Chapter 5 probably will not be relevant to you, but, again, may help inform you of the Canadian environment. If you are reading this book anywhere *in Canada, and are involved in genealogy as a hobby only*, Chapters 1, 3, 4, and 5 will be relevant to your activities. On the other hand, if you are *in the business of genealogy in Canada*, your work will involve you in Chapters 1, 2, 3, 4, and 5 — in other words, the whole book!

This book is based upon the law in Canada as of June 2009. Finally, it remains only to repeat that this book cannot substitute for legal advice. Please consult a lawyer qualified to practise in your province or territory to obtain specific legal opinions about specific situations that concern you.

CHAPTER I

Privacy and Personal Data Protection

Why might a genealogist be interested in questions of privacy and personal data protection? The answer to this lies in the changing environment in Canada, at least over the past quarter century, that has resulted in many of our jurisdictions passing laws related to the protection of privacy and personal data.

Vocabulary in this area is confusing. Many of the statutes, like the federal *Privacy Act*, contain the word "privacy" in their titles for legislation involving **personal data protection** — and many noted authorities and spokespeople also use "privacy" when discussing personal data protection. In five of our provinces, there are other statutes that deal directly with privacy in terms of being able to sue to force others to leave us alone in certain respects. In Newfoundland and Labrador, Manitoba, Saskatchewan, and British Columbia, these are called *Privacy Acts*. In Quebec, privacy protection is found in the provincial *Charter of Rights and Freedoms* as well as under the *Civil Code*. For this reason, among others, I will continue to refer to the laws with which we are concerned in this book as personal data protection statutes.

Privacy and Access to Information

Two different thrusts of legal activity have moved across Canada since 1977 and both of these affect the activity of genealogical research. First, there has been a movement toward making government-held information available to those who request it. Access-to-information laws mean that records held by government bodies have increasingly become available to genealogists requesting information.

There has been a parallel movement to protect individual privacy by protecting information that individuals provide about *themselves* to **organizations**. This second movement is potentially frustrating for genealogists because the information they seek is about *other* individuals. From the perspective of this area of the law, information about you is *your* information and information about other people is *their* information. Even information about other members of your family is considered private. Therefore, if personal data protection law is in effect in a particular situation, you will not be able to gain access to information about the other members of your family, never mind information about members of another family!

Barbara Turner Kinsella wrote in 2008 about her decades long search for her father. For much of that period, she was frustrated in every inquiry of government departments for information about the father she considered "missing" because the agencies would not answer her questions, citing data protection legislation. These agencies did not give her any information they may have held about her father because she was not her father. Finally, she did receive information about her father from a health provider (although this health provider presumably should have been bound by the same type of personal data protection legislation as others had cited) and, eventually, tracked him down. Unfortunately, the article had a bittersweet ending,

> *from its author's perspective, because her father had died shortly before she located him and there was information about him that she still was barred from accessing because of personal data protection law. On the other hand, her father had abandoned the family in her early childhood and had lived and died without apparently ever wishing to seek her out and his privacy was protected by the agencies with which he had come in contact during the many years prior to his death.*[1]

Evolution of Personal Data Protection

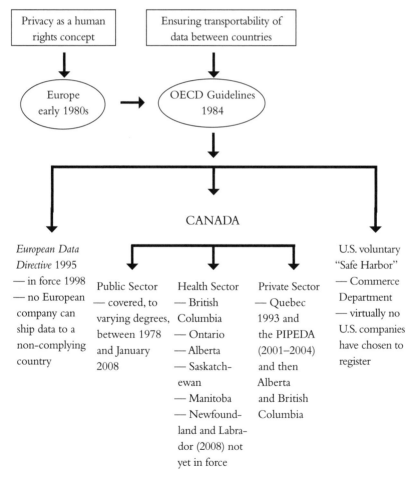

Exactly what information will be considered personal to an individual is defined in each personal data protection law in Canada. For example, under the *Personal Information Protection and Electronic Documents Act* [PIPEDA] of the federal government, in the case of private sector businesses, personal information is defined to mean any information about an identifiable individual but does not include the name, title, or business address or telephone number of any employee of any organization. By contrast, in Ontario, under the *Public Sector Salary Disclosure Act*, you can find the name, organization, and salary of any person working in the public sector and making a salary of over $100,000 because organizations are required to publish this list annually.

Records Held by Government

Various government organizations are now regulated by either **access-to-information** legislation or personal data protection legislation (often called "privacy" legislation) or both. The government organizations included in such legislation generally include government departments or ministries, frequently include municipal governments, and often include Crown corporations such as the Liquor Control Board of Ontario.

Personal data protection with respect to information held by bodies connected to the federal government was first legislated in 1977 under Part IV of the federal *Canadian Human Rights Act* but was later re-enacted as the *Privacy Act* in 1982. Indeed, in an unusual move, Parliament enacted two separate acts, the *Privacy Act* and the *Access to Information Act*, together as one bill. Two statutes is the model followed by New Brunswick. In Ontario, access and personal data protection have always been linked in legislation affecting government bodies: the *Freedom of*

Information and Protection of Privacy Act [FIPPA] was passed in 1987 and the *Municipal Freedom of Information and Protection of Privacy Act* [MFIPPA] in 1989. The combination has become the more common model in the other provinces and territories.

Each of the provinces and territories has its own access legislation governing the public sector and all have companion personal data protection legislation (listed below). Generally, however, it is clear in these laws that records that were specifically created by governments with the intention that they be made available to the public (such as land registry records) will continue to be made available even when they contain personally identifiable information about people. Although in Ontario this "grandfathered" public availability is phrased in general terms, in Quebec, for example, the personal data protection legislation is specifically stated in the law itself not to apply to land registry, civil status, or matrimonial regulations.

Provincial and Territorial Public Sector Access and Personal Data Protection Legislation

Alberta: *Freedom of Information and Protection of Privacy Act*, R.S.A. 2000, c. F–25

British Columbia: *Freedom of Information and Protection of Privacy Act*, R.S.B.C. 1996, c. 165

Manitoba: *Freedom of Information and Protection of Privacy Act*, S.M. 1997, c. 50

New Brunswick: *Protection of Personal Information Act*, S.N.B. 1978, c. P-19.1

New Brunswick: *Right to Information Act*, S.N.B. 1978, c. R-10.3

Newfoundland and Labrador: *Access to Information and Protection of Privacy Act*, S.N.L. 2002, c. A-1.1

Nova Scotia: *Freedom of Information and Protection of Privacy Act*, S.N.S. 1993, c. 5

Nunavut and Northwest Territories: *Access to Information and Protection of Privacy Act*, S.N.W.T. 1994, c. 20

Ontario: *Freedom of Information and Protection of Privacy Act*, R.S.O. 1990, c. F. 31

Ontario: *Municipal Freedom of Information and Protection of Privacy Act*, R.S.O. 1990, c. M 56

Prince Edward Island: *Freedom of Information and Protection of Privacy Act*, S.P.E.I. 2001, c. 37

Quebec: *An Act Respecting Access to Documents Held by Public Bodies and the Protection of Personal Information*, R.S.Q., c. A-2.1

Saskatchewan: *Freedom of Information and Protection of Privacy Act*, S.S. 1990-91, c. F-22.01

Saskatchewan: *Local Authority Freedom of Information and Protection of Privacy Act*, S.S. 1990-91, c. L-27.1

Yukon: *Access to Information and Protection of Privacy Act*, R.S.Y. 2002, c. 1

Personal data protection legislation creates a whole regime for the treatment of information about identifiable individuals from the moment that information is collected by an organization to the moment records containing that information are destroyed or deleted. This type of legislation regulates how an organization can collect information about individuals, how it should store it, how it must use it, how it must disseminate it to others outside the organization, and how it must dispose of it.

In the public sector, where personal data protection is linked to access legislation, if the **records** you seek are not protected by personal data protection laws or some other validly enacted exception to access, the organization is required to make them available to you. However, not every province and territory has decided to make every provincial and municipal organization subject to access legislation. Even the federal government lists the organizations subject to its access and personal data protection legislation and does not make every organization subject to these statutes. Organizations that are not subject to this legislation can choose whether or not to make any information, including personal data, available to you in your genealogical research.

Each act dealing with personal data protection in Canada has set a different time span on protection of the personally identifiable data held by organizations subject to it. Refer also to the table in Chapter 2, "Legislation and How Long Information Remains Confidential," on page 37.

- In Ontario, an organization subject to the *Freedom of Information and Protection of Privacy Act* or the *Municipal Freedom of Information and Protection of Privacy Act* must protect information about individuals for 30 years after that person's death.
- In Alberta, Saskatchewan, Prince Edward Island, and the Yukon, it is 25 years.
- In British Columbia, Nova Scotia, and under the federal public sector statute, it is 20 years. In the province of Newfoundland and Labrador, for historical purposes, it is the earlier of 20 years after death or 50 years after the record has been created.
- In Manitoba it is 10 years.
- Access legislation in New Brunswick is constructed differently.[2] Every exception to the right of access to the information held by the New Brunswick public sector organizations covered is permissive but not mandatory.[3] Therefore a government organization *can* refuse to release information about another person to a requestor but is not required to do so. Similarly, in Quebec, a government body can release personal information "to a [third party] person or a body where exceptional circumstances justify doing so."[4]

Once the fixed time periods legislated by the federal government and each province and territory for the protection of personally identifiable data held by public sector organizations have passed, that information must be made available to members of the public who request that information. Therefore, once the periods of protection for personally identifiable data held by public sector organizations in this country have expired, genealogists may request such information from public sector organizations and can expect to receive it.

On this reasoning, you might suppose that information held by the federal government from early censuses would gradually become available 20 years after the deaths of the individuals surveyed. However, the federal census-taking itself is governed by its own law. There is controversy about records of censuses taken after 1911 because, when taking these later, twentieth-century censuses, the government told those filling out the census that it would keep census information confidential.[5] Because no time limit was placed on this promise of confidentiality, the confidentiality promised eventually clashed with legislated time limits for public sector personal data protection legislated by Parliament much later in the twentieth century.[6] The federal government's solution, in the twenty-first century, has been to add a question to the 2006 census that asked members of households to consent to the release of information about themselves 92 years after the 2006 census.[7] The result is that there are years of the census from the twentieth century from which information will never be available to *current* genealogists except as combined data, because individual data from each census between 1911 and 2001 will only become available 92 years after that census was done.[8] And, furthermore, for at least the two census-takings beginning with the 2006 census, genealogists working 92 years from now will only be able to access the patchwork of records for those individuals who gave their

The Globe and Mail *has followed the movement of affected individuals to "opt out" of the new Ontario adoption information regime. See Erin Anderson, "Few People Push to Maintain Privacy as Ontario Set to Open Adoption Files,"* Globe and Mail, *26 May 2009; available at* www.theglobeandmail.com/news/national/opening-adoption -records-in-ontario-prompts-few-requests-for-secrecy/ article1152431.

consent to this access in the 2006 census and who decide to give it in the next census.[9] This patchwork of availability seems the likely situation for all future censuses.[10]

Another area of the law where general personal data protection legislation has been overridden in some instances by specific statutory provisions is in the context of adoption records. In June 2009, Ontario's new *Access to Adoption Records Act* came into force. The act dramatically alters the data protection environment for these records in Ontario, bringing it into line with similar laws already in place in British Columbia, Alberta, Manitoba, and

Patchwork Problems in Other Countries

An editorial in a U.S.-based Jewish genealogical association newsletter details similar problems with patchwork legislation in the United States. Concerned with the limited access to information inherent in data protection laws, it discusses whether enforcement techniques often only hinder honest attempts to access data while doing little against determined illegal access. Detailing a personal experience of the author, two branches of a family, separated during the Holocaust, were reunited because of information available in California. If the family had lived in New Jersey, on the other hand, the discovery of the missing family members would never have occurred because New Jersey has stricter data protection legislation.[11]

Newfoundland and Labrador. This legislation allows birth parents and adopted children access to previously inaccessible, "sealed" adoption records so they can locate each other.

Paradoxically, this legislation may make it easier for children and parents involved in adoptions to locate their parents and children, respectively, than for children and parents not involved in adoptions to locate each other once they have lost track of each other.

Records Held in the Private Sector

Until 2004, personal data protection legislation in Canada (except Quebec) affected only government bodies. In 2004, a new piece of legislation, which the federal government had passed in 2001, came into full effect: the *Personal Information Protection and Electronic Documents Act* [PIPEDA]. This statute has signalled a new era in Canada — personal data protection is now an obligation imposed on private sector organizations as well as on public sector ones. Indeed, because PIPEDA applies to all organizations engaged in commercial activities, it is possible that we now have a greater scope for personal data protection in the private sector in Canada than in the public. This situation will probably not persist for long. In Ontario, for example, universities were originally not covered by either the *Freedom of Information and Protection of Privacy Act* or the *Municipal Freedom of Information and Protection of Privacy Act* but the McGuinty provincial government (elected in 2003, re-elected in 2007) brought them all under the *Freedom of Information and Protection of Privacy Act* in 2006.

There is no corresponding *access* legislation covering information held in private sector organizations. This means that, although private sector organizations are legally obliged to protect information about identifiable individuals, there is no requirement on a private sector organization in Canada, even after personal data protection time periods have expired, to make any information available to anyone. This will probably signal a general tightening up for genealogists of information held by private sector organizations in Canada.

Federally regulated businesses in Canada, such as airlines and those in the banking industry, as well as businesses in certain provinces and territories (the Maritimes, Saskatchewan, Manitoba, and Ontario) must comply with PIPEDA. Because the constitutional ability of our federal Parliament to pass such a sweeping statute governing the whole business sector in Canada is in some doubt, the federal government has left room for the provinces to pass their own, similar, legislation for the private sector. Quebec already had such legislation, which has been deemed equivalent to PIPEDA. British Columbia and Alberta have followed suit with their own statutes, also deemed equivalent. Thus private sector organizations in Quebec, British Columbia, and Alberta must generally comply with their respective provincial statutes and not with PIPEDA.

Health information is a particular category of personal information that has fallen under a variety of provincial laws as well as, in some respects, under PIPEDA. This is an area of changing laws in Canada and genealogists may wish to keep up to date on changes in this area in the future. (An excellent source is the website of the Privacy Commissioner of Canada at *www.priv.gc.ca/index_e.cfm*.) Some provinces have enacted specific legislation to deal with personal health information.

Provincial Health Information Legislation

Alberta: *Health Information Act*, R.S.A. 2000, c. H-5
British Columbia: *E-Health (Personal Health Information Access and Protection of Privacy) Act*, S.B.C. 2008, c. 38
Manitoba: *Personal Health Information Act*, C.C.S.M., c. PP33.5

Newfoundland and Labrador: *Personal Health Information Act*, S.N.L. 2008, c. P-7.01 (not in force as of June 2009)
Ontario: *Personal Health Information Act*, 2004, S.O. 2004, c. 3, Sch. A
Saskatchewan: *Health Information Protection Act*, S.S. 1999, c. H-0.021

- In Ontario, the *Personal Health Information Protection Act* [PHIPA] is specific legislation passed by the Ontario Legislature that has also been approved by the federal government as equivalent to PIPEDA for most of the health sector (for health information custodians, as defined in the Ontario statute). Organizations subject to this act need only comply with it and not with the federal PIPEDA.

- In Alberta, there is a *Health Information Act* that has not been deemed equivalent to PIPEDA at the federal level and so the private sector organizations affected must currently comply with both Alberta's HIA and PIPEDA. Public sector organizations covered by HIA need comply only with HIA.

- A similar situation to that in Alberta currently exists for Manitoba's *Personal Health Information Act* [PHIA], Saskatchewan's *Health Information Protection Act* [HIPA], and British Columbia's E-Health Act (*Personal Health Information Access and Protection of Privacy*): all have passed and are in effect but are not deemed equivalent to PIPEDA. Thus private sector health organizations in Manitoba, Saskatchewan, and British Columbia need to comply both with the provincial health information legislation and PIPEDA while public sector organizations are governed only by the provincial health information legislation.

- Newfoundland and Labrador has passed a statute, the *Personal Health Information Act*, that has not yet come into force (and has not been deemed equivalent to PIPEDA by the federal government) but, when it does come into force in Newfoundland and Labrador, both it and PIPEDA will have an effect on genealogists seeking certain materials from that province.

All this legislation is relevant to those genealogists who might be searching for hospital records. I have been asked questions by people, for example, seeking to know whether their relatives have spent time in the tuberculosis sanitariums in Ontario. In general, because of this legislation and older law relating to medical records, such information is only available to patients (and, in some cases, their legal representatives).

Access, Privacy, and Genealogical Research

If you are trying to find out about someone and you know that a number of public and private sector organizations in Canada may hold information about this person, you can apply to any organization that you believe might have records, any selection of them, or all of them. It is a common practice to apply to more than one organization. Since personal data protection and access legislation differs from province to province and between territories and federal legislation, what is not released to you from one organization may be made available to you from another. You may not get the original letter from the organization that holds it, but you may get a copy of it from another.

In most jurisdictions, if you are acting as agent for the legally appointed personal representative or executor of a person who has died and you are within the number of years that jurisdiction protects personal data held by organizations, you can insist that the personal information about that person be released to you. You can also help a person to whom information relates to apply to an organization governed by personal data protection legislation for information about her- or himself. You cannot, however, represent yourself as agent for people with whom you have no direct connection. For example, you cannot represent yourself as acting as agent for a granddaughter in applying for information about her just because you are working on a genealogy of your family that includes her.

Curiously there is no provision for a deceased's legal representative to act after death regarding personal information under PIPEDA. So, it would appear that during the 20 years following an individual's death that PIPEDA applies to that person, organizations covered by PIPEDA will be unable to release information about that individual to anyone at all (if the record in question is under 100 years old). Under the federal public sector *Privacy Act*, there *is* a specific provision providing for access by the deceased's legally appointed personal representative or executor — but only for purposes of administration of the estate, not for genealogy.

Personal data protection in the public sector in Canada is largely complaint-driven. That is, under the statutes, the person whose information has been wrongly handled by the organization involved can complain. At the federal level and in Ontario, British Columbia, Alberta, Newfoundland and Labrador, and Prince Edward Island there are Commissioners to whom the complaint is made (although in Newfoundland and Labrador, the person concerned can choose to go to court instead of to the Commissioner).

In Quebec, there is a Commission. In Manitoba and New Brunswick complaints are handled through the provinces' Ombudspersons — but New Brunswick also offers the alternative of going to court. In Nova Scotia, a complaint may be taken either to the Review Officer appointed under its *Freedom of Information and Protection of Privacy Act* or to court.

At the federal level (and in Manitoba, Saskatchewan,

Newfoundland and Labrador, New Brunswick, and Nova Scotia), the Commissioner (or other complaints investigator created under that province's statute) must investigate the complaint against a public sector organization covered by the legislation but then can only make a recommendation. With respect to the federal *Privacy Act*, if the public sector organization involved does not comply with the Commissioner's recommendation, the Commissioner may take the matter to the courts. At the federal level, the Privacy Commissioner is a separate office from the Information Commissioner whereas, in the provinces, the roles are combined. In some cases the federal Privacy Commissioner and the federal Information Commissioner (who is focused on public access to government information) have taken different positions before the Federal Court.

In Alberta, British Columbia, Ontario, Prince Edward Island, and Quebec, the decisions of the Commissioners or other reviewing appointees are final and determinative of the complaint. In these provinces, the courts will only become involved if one of the parties to the complaint formally appeals the decision by the Commissioner or other complaints decision-maker under the statutes (or, of course, in New Brunswick, Newfoundland and Labrador, and Nova Scotia if the complainant decides to go directly to the courts for relief, as mentioned above).

With respect to Ontario's public sector legislation, the Ontario Commissioner him- or herself has legally binding decision-making power — but the individual involved in making the complaint will not receive direct compensation (that is, money) for breaches of the statute. As is evident from the description here about who decides when a complaint is launched in a given jurisdiction, each province and territory has set up its own mechanism to handle violations of its personal data protection regime or regimes.

The Ontario Commissioner's Office recently released a decision involving genealogical research.12 The adjudicator found that the names, grades, and dates of students' attendance at a school are the personal information of the students. As well, the teachers' names are also personal as part of their employment history. Nevertheless, the information requested that involved students and teachers who died before 1979 was found to not be covered by the Ontario personal data protection legislation and thus would be accessible to a genealogist requesting it from the public sector school board that held it. The adjudicator also dealt with the problem the school board then faced about how to know who had died by 1979 in a large group of photos. The adjudicator looked at life expectancy data produced by Statistics Canada for the relevant period and decided the Board must release, under its legislated access mandate, information on those born before 1919. Endeavouring to gain access to information about those in the pictures born after 1919 as well, the genealogist making the request argued that he was engaged in "research." The Commissioner's Office agreed that genealogy is research but held that it did not comply with the statutory conditions of the research exception to personal data protection — that the research meet security and confidentiality conditions — and thus, although engaged in research, the genealogist was not given access to information about students or teachers whose information was still governed by the legislation (those born after 1919).

The federal private sector personal data protection regime, however, legislates different consequences for breach than exist in the federal public sector *Privacy Act* context we have just mentioned. Under PIPEDA, as under the federal *Privacy Act*, the federal Privacy Commissioner must investigate the complaint made and must then make a recommendation. However, under PIPEDA, once the report of the Privacy Commissioner has been issued, either the Commissioner or the complainant can take the organization being complained about to the Federal Court. At this point, it is open to the Court, if the complaint is judged to be well-founded, to order, among other things, that the organization involved pay damages (that is, money) to the complainant. This provision makes the risk of non-compliance to a private sector organization governed by PIPEDA different (and some would say, greater) than the risk to public sector organizations in Canada that are governed by public sector personal data protection.

If you are working on genealogy as a private individual, you are not an organization covered by any personal data protection rules in Canada and so you are quite entitled to include information about any individuals, living or dead, in your genealogy *once you have the information.* This is because PIPEDA does not apply to "any individual in respect of information that the individual collects, uses or discloses for personal or domestic purposes and does not collect, use or disclose for any other purpose."[13] (As discussed earlier, you may be affected by the personal data protection legislation that governs organizations from which you are trying to get information – but once you have information in your possession, you yourself do not have to comply with any personal data protection legislation in your use and dessimination of any information you have.)

Nothing in personal data protection legislation stops you, as an individual working on your own family tree or, as a hobby, on anyone else's family trees, from publishing your personally created family histories. This assumes, of course, that you avoid libelling the living (see Chapter 5)! It is another paradox in our evolving law about information that you cannot libel dead people but the dead have "privacy" rights under personal data protection regimes in this country for a number of years after death. There may be other legal barriers to publication of your personally created family histories, discussed in Chapter 4 on copyright, if you used commercial software in the creation of the genealogy or include copies of documents created by other parties.

CHAPTER 2

The Business of Genealogy

Genealogy as a Hobby and as a Profession

Genealogists working in Canada who are paid for their efforts have to comply with different legal requirements than those genealogists engaged in the same activities for free. This chapter explains why this difference exists and how "professional" genealogists are affected by legislation that does not apply to their "amateur" counterparts.

An amateur genealogist who turns an unpaid hobby into a commercial activity, such as doing a paid genealogy for a distant relative that relies, at least in part, on the unpaid research done as a hobby, may find that turning to commercial activities brings her or his efforts under personal data protection legislation. This would not retroactively affect the work done while pursuing strictly non-commercial, private pursuits. But it might require that work be re-done, to adhere to the requirements of the personal data protection legislation, when the "commercial activity" is undertaken — because that activity would require adherence to all the provisions of the personal data protection legislation that will be discussed here in connection with the activities of professional genealogists. Turning unpaid, hobby genealogy into a book should not require the amateur genealogist to adhere to the requirements of the personal data protection statutes because journalistic and literary efforts are exempted from personal data protection law.

As discussed in Chapter 1, both amateur and professional genealogists, in their efforts to locate sources, may be affected by the personal data protection requirements placed on the individuals and organizations from which they seek information. On the other hand, in their own information-handling practices, although amateur genealogists do not need to comply with this type of legislation while working with information in their own hands as they undertake their own genealogical research, professional genealogists do.

Personal data protection legislation is an area of law that is relatively new in Canada. Over approximately the past quarter-century, public sector organizations such as hospitals, schools, government offices, and many Crown corporations and police forces have become subject to laws protecting information about personally identifiable individuals. Genealogists have increasingly encountered this phenomenon when seeking information about individuals from such sources and, as described in Chapter 1, will continue to do so.

At the same time, this increasing protection of personally identifiable information held by public sector organizations has been paired in all cases with access legislation. This means that these same public organizations are required to give members of the public access to information — unless the information concerns personally identifiable individuals or is subject to other legislated exceptions that would compel or permit the organization to keep the information a secret. Thus, personal data protection legislation, often referred to as privacy legislation, has evolved in Canada mostly in the context of an overall environment of governments providing access to information held in public sector organizations.

There are no *access*-to-information rights applicable in the private sector as exist in the public sector. Private sector organizations and individuals can choose, at their own option, whether and when to provide or withhold information that an outsider might request. There *is*, however, increasingly a requirement (mentioned in Chapter 1) that organizations, and especially businesses, in the private sector provide personal data protection.

Since private sector organizations are not required to provide *access* to information and since personal data protection legislation generally requires businesses to prevent personal data from leaving the organization (except to the person who is the subject of the information), genealogists generally are experiencing an overall reluctance by private sector organizations to give out information.

This chapter deals not with the experience of genealogists in getting other organizations to provide information but with the legal requirements that are now placed upon how the *professional* genealogist handles her or his own information related to genealogy throughout every aspect of her or his research. The discussion will focus on the provisions of the federal PIPEDA, both because most of the country is governed by PIPEDA and because Ontario, home of the Ontario Genealogical Society, is governed by PIPEDA. Professional genealogists in Saskatchewan, Manitoba, New Brunswick, Nova Scotia, Prince Edward Island, Newfoundland and Labrador, and the three territories would also look to PIPEDA. The structure of the personal data protection legislation applying to the private sector in the other three Canadian jurisdictions is very like the structure of PIPEDA. Professional genealogists in Alberta will look to its *Personal*

Information Protection Act and in British Columbia to its *Personal Information Protection Act.*

Professional genealogists in Quebec will be governed by *An Act Respecting the Protection of Personal Information in the Privacy Sector.* This statute provides that its object

> is to establish, for the exercise of the rights conferred by articles 35 to 40 of the Civil Code of Quebec concerning the protection of personal information, particular rules with respect to personal information relating to other persons which a person collects, holds, uses or communicates to third persons in the course of carrying on an enterprise with the meaning of article 1525 of the Civil Code of Quebec.[1]

However, in the only direct reference to genealogy in any personal data protection statute in Canada, the Quebec statute provides further that "[t]his Act does not apply to journalistic, historical or genealogical material collected, held, used or communicated for the legitimate information of the public." It might at first glance seem, then, that professional genealogists in Quebec need not conform to the requirements of *An Act Respecting the Protection of Personal Information in the Private Sector* — but, on second consideration, this latter phrase ("for the legitimate information of the public") should give professional genealogists pause before assuming that they are not subject to Quebec's private sector personal data protection statute. In completing a genealogy for a private client, it would seem very difficult to argue that the genealogical material gathered by the Quebec professional genealogist was done for the information of the public rather than as a purely private commissioned activity.

As noted in Chapter 1, in British Columbia, Alberta, Manitoba, Saskatchewan, and Ontario the provincial legislatures have taken the development of personal data protection law a step further and provided separate systems of protection in the health sector (and similar legislation has been passed in Newfoundland and Labrador but is not yet in force in the province). For most health-related information, genealogists seeking material held by Ontario organizations would only need to consult the health-sector legislation because this legislation replaces both the public sector provincial personal data protection legislation for this material and the federal PIPEDA. In the other provinces, while the health sector personal data protection legislation replaces the provincial *public* sector general personal data protection legislation with respect to this material, the federal PIPEDA legislation is still also applicable to health information held by private sector organizations. This special area of health-related personal data protection legislation will only affect professional genealogists in Canada who seek information from health-related organizations (in the same way that it will affect those working in genealogy as a hobby): if a professional genealogist *acquires* health-related information, that information should be treated by the genealogist in the same way as the other personal information that she or he has acquired (under PIPEDA or the equivalent, in those provinces where PIPEDA has been replaced by provincial legislation — Quebec, British Columbia, and Alberta).

The amateur genealogist falls outside the purview of the new requirements for private sector personal data protection in her or his own acquiring, using, storing, and disseminating of personal information in the course of genealogical activities because PIPEDA specifically provides that "[it] does not apply to ... any individual in respect of information that the individual collects, uses or discloses for personal or domestic purposes and does not collect, use or disclose for any other purpose."[2] And, as well, an amateur genealogist is not paid for her or his genealogical activities and thus cannot be considered to be in business.

A professional genealogist, on the other hand, *is* paid for her or his services and does not work with personal data for "personal or domestic purposes" but rather is engaged in "commercial activity," which in PIPEDA is defined as "any particular transaction, act or conduct or any regular course of conduct that is of a commercial character."

It is true that PIPEDA focuses on "organizations" engaged in commercial activities — and many professional genealogists do not ordinarily consider themselves to be part of organizations — but PIPEDA provides its own unique definition of an **"organization"**[3] and that definition means that organizations includes associations, partnerships, and individual persons — in short, PIPEDA applies to any genealogy enterprise being undertaken as a business. Any professional genealogist, whether working alone, as part of a firm, with a partner, or in a company, will find him- or herself needing to adhere to the requirements of this legislation. Similarly, professional genealogists working in Canadian jurisdictions where PIPEDA does not apply (as discussed earlier) will find themselves subject to that jurisdiction's particular private sector personal data protection laws.

Professional genealogists in Canada are required to observe this legislation while professional writers are not. This is because PIPEDA provides that it "does not apply to … any organization in respect of personal information that the organization collects, uses or discloses for journalistic, artistic or literary purposes and does not collect, use or disclose for any other purpose."[4]

This legislation affects professional genealogists in Canada but this type of legislation is virtually unknown in the United States. Nevertheless, *all* information about identifiable individuals gathered and dealt with from any part of the world by professional genealogists working *in* Canada will need to be considered in terms of the relevant private sector personal data protection legislation — not just information gathered about Canadians or from Canadian sources.

What Information Is Affected?

Doing genealogy as a business requires a genealogist to work with information that is the quintessential focus of personal data protection legislation. As defined by PIPEDA, "'personal information' means any information about an identifiable individual, but does not include the name, title or business address or telephone number of any employee of an organization."[5]

Just about every personal detail that makes a genealogy interesting or worthwhile to a professional genealogist would fall within the area governed by the legislation: age, marital status, race, religion, education, employment history, or personal financial information, for example.

On the other hand, not *every* individual will be a person whose information is protected by this legislation. Persons who have been dead for some time were not of interest to our legislators in this respect. It is one of the peculiarities of this new area of Canadian law that various legislatures have deemed individuals' personal data to be protected for differing periods of time after their deaths:

- PIPEDA requires that organizations protect information about individuals for 20 years after their deaths — or until the records containing the information are themselves over 100 years old, whichever is the earlier.

- In the Alberta statute, the period of protection after death is exactly the same as PIPEDA.

- In Quebec, the period of protection is 30 years after death or in a document until it is 100 years old.

- In the British Columbia statute, the situation is a little more subtle: information may be released from an organization about an individual who has been dead 20 or more years or where the record containing the information is more than 100 years old — but only in cases where the information is to be used for archival or historical purposes. It would seem logical that genealogical research could be considered historical.

Legislation and How Long
Information Remains Confidential

Federal *Privacy Act* (public sector)	20 years after death — and then the information falls out of the Act
PIPEDA (private sector)	May disclose 20 years after individual's death, or, if shorter, 100 years after record made
Ontario FOIPPA & MFOIPPA	30 years after death, out of Act
Alberta, Saskatchewan, Prince Edward Island	25 years after death, accessible
British Columbia, Nova Scotia	20 years after death, accessible
Manitoba	10 years after death, accessible
New Brunswick, Quebec	Never accessible as of right now, but always discretionary

Collection of Information about Living or Recently Deceased Persons

The biggest obstacle here for professional genealogy would seem to be that "[t]he knowledge and consent of the individual are required for the collection, use or disclosure of personal information, except where inappropriate."[6]

Normally, a client of a professional genealogist is requesting information about other members of the client's family — what clients want to learn from the professional genealogist is information about other personally identifiable individuals. From the perspective of the law, information about family members does not "belong" to the client, it is information about *other* personally identifiable individuals — each of whom is entitled to the protection of the legislation when there is a professional genealogist involved. The client can only consent to collection of information directly about the client him- or herself — but not about any other member of the family. In order to collect information about other living members of the client's family, the professional genealogist will require the consent of those other family members. As PIPEDA phrases this, a professional genealogist "may collect personal information without the knowledge or consent of the individual only if ... the collection is clearly in the interests of the individual and consent cannot be obtained in a timely way."[7]

Tracking Down Donor 188

Waterloo resident Rob Hunter has spent more than a year attempting to identify his biological father who was the donor of the sperm that was used in Mr. Hunter's conception. After months of attempting to access information about the donor, he has only managed to learn the donor's three-digit ID number and a small list of physical characteristics:

the donor's height, weight, approximate age at donation, and a familial history of hypertension on the donor's father's side. Beyond that, personal data protection legislation that now governs the organization that holds the records prevents the release of anything more detailed. Also, the donor had requested and was promised complete confidentiality.[8]

Although genealogy is a fascinating and absorbing study — and it is evident that a client would see collection of information about family members as being in the interests of the client, at least, if not of the other family members — other family members cannot be presumed to value the genealogy exercise as highly. Since there is rarely any urgency to the quest for a client's roots, it is not possible to argue that the consent of other family members to the collection of information about them could not be obtained in a timely way. Hence, professional genealogists must have the knowledge and consent of other family members in order to collect information about them.

Even if other family members consent, PIPEDA provides that the collection should be directly from those individuals: information about Aunt Mabel should be from Aunt Mabel, herself, and not from Grandmother Mary about Aunt Mabel, or even from publicly available sources. PIPEDA provides that "[e]ven publicly available information is to be collected by a PIPEDA-governed organization only if it is so specified in the Regulations."[9]

The sources specified in the regulations as available for gathering information about an individual from whom consent has *not* been received are:

> (a) [information] … in a telephone directory that is available to the public, where the subscriber can refuse to have the personal information appear in the directory;

(b) [information] … in a professional or business directory, listing or notice, that is available to the public, where the collection, use and disclosure of the personal information relate directly to the purpose for which the information appears in the directory, listing or notice;

(c) [information] … in a registry collected under a statutory authority and to which a right of public access is authorized by law, where the collection, use and disclosure of the personal information relate directly to the purpose for which the information appears in the registry;

(d) [information] … in a record or document of a judicial or quasi-judicial body, that is available to the public, where the collection, use and disclosure of the personal information relate directly to the purpose for which the information appears in the record or document; and

(e) [information] … in a publication, including a magazine, book or newspaper, in printed or electronic form, that is available to the public, where the individual has provided the information.

Thus, the professional genealogist in Canada might gather information about those family members, such as information on businesses or occupations, from telephone and other directories and land registries and so on without the consent of other family members. Nevertheless, there may be some concern as a result of PIPEDA's requirement that any information gathered from such sources must be used for a purpose relating directly to the purpose for which the information was provided in the directory or registry.

Since the professional genealogist's purpose is to provide a family history to the client, the purposes of the professional genealogist and the purposes for which the directories and registries exist may not be considered to be compatible. Therefore, a professional genealogist would always be safer to have the consent of the person to whom the information relates before gathering the data from any source.

Collecting, using, or passing along information provided in obituaries would appear to be problematic for the professional genealogist. Such information would certainly be information "in a publication, including a magazine, book or newspaper, in printed or electronic form, that is available to the public" as would be required to fit into the exception set out on page 40 as (e) — but that exception goes on to require that "the individual has provided the information" — and, for obvious reasons, that is not usually the case in an obituary. (The question of reproducing obituaries and other newspaper announcements, as distinct from taking information from them, will be dealt with in Chapter 4, which discusses copyright issues, and Chapter 5 discusses some instances where living persons have been libelled in obituaries!)

The Internet and digitization means that information about individuals abounds in an ever-increasing number of sources. However, personal data protection legislation means that the professional genealogist should not use these, or other available sources, to obtain information about living people (unless, perhaps, they have given their permission to do so) — because the professional genealogist, bound by the legislation, is required to get the information directly from the person in whom she or he is interested.

Curiously, as mentioned in Chapter 1, under PIPEDA there does not seem to be any person who can access information after the death of an individual and before the shorter of the 100 years after creation of the record or the 20 years after the death. By contrast, the *Privacy Act* specifically provides that in the interim period between the death of an individual and the public access to the individual's information (which follows, when a public sector institution is involved, because of the access provisions of the legislation), there is extremely limited access to the information about the deceased individual. Only the deceased's legally appointed personal representative or executor can access information about the deceased, and then only for purposes of the administration of the estate. There are no similar provisions in PIPEDA.

How Information about Individuals Can Be Used

When a professional genealogist wants to use information that falls within the scope of personal data protection legislation, how is he or she affected? The legislation requires that the professional genealogist adhere to specific requirements regarding the treatment of that information with respect to its collection, use, dissemination, and disposal. In other words, when information about an identifiable individual comes within the scope of this legislation, its entire "life cycle" in the hands of the professional genealogist will be affected.

Once a professional genealogist has gathered information about an identifiable individual, his or her responsibilities to comply with personal data protection legislation last as long as the information continues to be identifiable with the individual. For example, if a professional genealogist gathered information about all French-speaking descendents of an eighteenth-century émigré now living in a particular town (with permissions from each of them to do so) and then aggregated that information to produce a report about the French-speaking population of the town — and the report no longer contained any identification of particular individuals who would be entitled to personal data protection (nothing that could connect any particular individual now living or recently deceased with the general information being provided, nothing like names, addresses, or uniquely identifiable occupations), that report could be distributed and shared by the professional genealogist without any further concerns about personal data protection legislation. The underlying individual records about the descendants who are living or deceased within the time frames of the personal data protection statute, however, that remained in the professional genealogist's office would continue to be subject to the strictures of the legislation. This responsibility holds whether or not the individuals whom the information concerns are aware or ever become aware that the professional genealogist holds this information.

If a professional genealogist gathers information about Aunt Helen from Aunt Helen for the purpose of providing a genealogy to a client, Aunt Gita, that information cannot be subsequently used by that professional genealogist to inform a genealogy being prepared for Uncle Sayd. To use that information in the genealogy for Uncle Sayd, the professional genealogist would have to go back to Aunt Helen and get consent for that new purpose. If the original consent was given to use the information in constructing *any* genealogy involving Aunt Helen, the second use would already have been covered by the original consent and no further approach to Aunt Helen would be necessary. Personally identifiable information can only be used by the professional genealogist for the purposes for which consent was given by the subject of that information.

How and When Can Professional Genealogists Give Information to Others?

The provision that may most affect the work of the professional genealogist is the requirement that professional genealogists give the information they have gathered about living individuals to those individuals, should they request it, according to clause 4.9 of Schedule 1 to PIPEDA. If the individual wants a copy of the record that contains the information, the professional genealogist is obliged to permit the individual to make a copy of it — even if that record is under copyright. No matter who has copyright interests in a particular record, copyright will not apply in the case of a copy made by a professional genealogist to fulfil a request made of him or her pursuant to personal data protection legislation because the federal government amended the Canadian *Copyright Act* to say so explicitly. It does not matter where the record was made — in Canada or elsewhere — what matters is that it is held in Canada by a professional genealogist. If the person requesting the copy of the record turns around and begins to use the record in ways that infringe the rights of the copyright holder in the record (making multiple copies or translating the document or posting it on the Internet, for example), the copyright holder will be able to enforce the copyright fully against that person, but not against the professional genealogist. (See Chapter 4 for further discussion of copyright.)

If the record in question contains information about a number of individuals, including the person asking for it, the professional genealogist will have to make a copy available to the person making the request on which the genealogist has "blacked out" all the personally identifiable information except the information about the individual making the request. The obligation to make a copy of a record for the person who is the subject of the record, on request to the professional genealogist is not a matter involving compensating the professional genealogist for professional services — there need be no contract between the professional genealogist and the person requesting the information from the professional genealogist. This is a question of individuals' rights to access information about themselves held by businesses that are subject to the personal data protection legislation. Therefore, the professional genealogist must make this information available to a requestor — and any compensation that the professional genealogist wants for making the information available must be in line with the fees that are permitted under the regulations to the personal data protection legislation.

Certainly, without explicit permission from all those whose personal information is covered by personal data protection legislation (the living and those who have died relatively recently, as described previously), genealogies cannot be posted to the Internet or otherwise published by professional genealogists working in Canada. This is because, although not yet tested in court, it is unlikely that genealogies themselves would qualify as literary, artistic, or journalistic works that fall outside the requirements of the personal data protection legislation, as pointed out earlier. There may also be copyright consequences to publishing or posting genealogical charts and information created using proprietary software, as will be discussed in Chapter 4.

Is It Possible to "Get Around" Personal Data Protection Requirements?

Some have argued that an "agency agreement" between the professional genealogist, as agent, and the client, as principal, would give the professional genealogist status as making "personal or domestic use" of the information used in the research. It would be as if the professional genealogist *were* the client making personal or domestic use of genealogical information. Thus, it is argued, the professional genealogist would not be engaged in "commercial activity" and would not be bound by personal data protection legislation.

This agency idea may have arisen because there have been cases where one person has been successful in acting as agent for another individual in requesting access to information from public sector institutions. Commentators have denounced this practice and it seems very unlikely that a court would view an agency arrangement as absolving the professional genealogist of all responsibility to adhere to the requirements of personal data protection legislation.

First, PIPEDA makes no provision for an affected organization to act as agent for any other party. Each organization that deals with personally identifiable information must comply with the legislation — the legislation even contemplates information about people moving from organization to organization and assumes that each organization will comply — not that one will comply and subsequent ones, acting pursuant to an agency relationship with the first, will not have to comply themselves. Second, doctors and lawyers act as agents professionally for individuals in many instances and both groups of professionals are considered to be governed by personal data protection legislation, with no possibility of being considered outside its scope by virtue of agency relationships agreed between themselves and their patients or clients. Given these realities, it is unlikely that genealogists will be able to successfully avoid the requirements of personal data protection legislation through these creative arrangements.

What Are the Consequences of Ignoring Personal Data Protection Legislation?

There do not appear to be any cases to date in which the activities of a professional genealogist have been investigated or pursued by the federal Privacy Commissioner in Canada (or under the Quebec, Alberta, or British Columbia legislation). However, the possibility of running into difficulty if personal data protection legislation is ignored by professional genealogists certainly exists. A person who believes that a professional genealogist in Canada has mishandled personally identifiable information "[c]an file with the [federal Privacy] Commissioner a written complaint against [the professional genealogist] for contravening a provision of [PIPEDA] or for not following a recommendation set out in Schedule 1 [to PIPEDA]."[10] It is the person who is the subject of the information who has the right to complain: one person cannot make a complaint on behalf of another. For example, if Matilda feels aggrieved about the information practices of a professional genealogist, Matilda can complain, but Sam cannot complain about information involving Matilda.

As well, even without any complaint being formally launched, "[i]f the Commissioner is satisfied that there are reasonable grounds to investigate a matter …, the Commissioner may initiate a complaint in respect of the matter."[11]

In either of these cases, once an investigation is completed under PIPEDA, the federal Privacy Commissioner can make public the results of the investigation — but the Commissioner cannot issue any binding order. Matters can be taken from the Commissioner to the Federal Court, which does have the power to issue binding orders and, in appropriate proceedings, can order an offending professional genealogist to pay damages to a complainant. Although the Commissioner's findings may not, in themselves, be enforceable against a professional genealogist, the Commissioner's powers to investigate a complaint have teeth. Those holding information that is the subject of a request under PIPEDA must not dispose of that information for as long as an individual who feels aggrieved at the outcome of a request for that information is pursuing remedies under PIPEDA and those subject to PIPEDA must not obstruct the Commissioner in an investigation or an information audit of the business. The penalties for so doing range from fines of up to $10,000 on conviction of a summary offence to $100,000 for an indictable offence.

CHAPTER 3

Cemeteries as Sources of Genealogical Information

Cemeteries are excellent sources for genealogical information. Genealogists have been active in preserving this information by taking a keen interest in preserving and caring for cemeteries. This is the subject of "The Ontario Genealogical Society and The Cemeteries Act" by Marjorie Stuart, published in 2002 in *Families*, the journal of the Ontario Genealogical Society.[1] Genealogists have also been active in exploiting the information that cemeteries contain.

This chapter will address the law relating to this second genealogical interest — the information opportunities to be found in cemeteries. The discussion is based on law current to June 2009, as mentioned earlier. There is a new Ontario statute, the *Funeral, Burial and Cremation Services Act, 2002*, that has been passed by the Ontario Legislature but has yet to be proclaimed in force. It will then replace the current *Cemeteries Act (Revised)*, [hereinafter, the *Cemeteries Act*]. Since it is not possible to know when the new *Funeral, Burial and Cremation Services Act*, 2002 will be proclaimed in force, and given the number of years that have already passed without the proclamation, this chapter will focus on the *Cemeteries Act* in describing the law in Ontario.

The Governance of Cemeteries

In Canada, provinces have the authority to enact laws concerning cemeteries. There is no role for the federal government in the regulation of cemeteries except those cemeteries that are connected to matters constitutionally designated as lying exclusively within the powers of the federal government, such as the Canadian Armed Forces cemeteries. Thus there are military cemeteries that are governed by federal regulation. Provincial cemetery legislation varies widely across the country. See the list below. Newfoundland and Labrador does not appear to have specific legislation for cemeteries like that found in the other provinces. In Quebec, the *Burial Act* is silent with respect to access to cemeteries but specifically grants the Roman Catholic Church the right to refuse burial in consecrated ground for any reason. The *Non-Catholic Cemeteries Act* places these cemeteries under the authority of the Quebec Minister of Health and Social Services but is, again, silent on the topic of access to these cemeteries.

This chapter will focus on the situation in Ontario, but references will be made to other provinces.

Cemeteries can be owned by private businesses, such as the Mount Pleasant Group of Cemeteries that owns and operates Mount Pleasant Cemetery in Toronto. They can also be affiliated with religious organizations, such as the Roman Catholic Diocese of London with which St. Peter's Cemetery in London is connected.[2] Finally, cemeteries can be part of municipalities,[3] such as those owned and operated by the City of Niagara Falls.[4] Under the Ontario *Cemeteries Act*, abandoned cemeteries also become the responsibility of the municipalities in which they are situated.[5]

Provincial Legislation Relating to Cemeteries

Alberta: *Cemeteries Act*, R.S.A. 2000, c. C-3

British Columbia: *Cremation, Internment and Funeral Services Act*, S.B.C. 2004, c. 35

Manitoba: *Cemeteries Act*, C.C.S.M. c. C30

New Brunswick: *Cemetery Companies Act*, R.S.N.B. 1973, c. C-1

Nova Scotia: *Cemetery and Funeral Services Act*, R.S.N.S. 1989, c. 62

Nova Scotia: *Cemeteries Protection Act*, S.N.S. 1998, c. 9

Ontario: *Cemeteries Act (Revised)*, R.S.O. 1990, c. C.4

Ontario: *Funeral, Burial and Cremation Services Act, 2002*, S.O. 2002, c. 33 (Not yet in force as of August 2009)

Prince Edward Island: *Cemeteries Act*, R.S.P.E.I. 1988, c. C-2

Quebec: *Burial Act*, R.S.Q. c. I-11

Quebec: *Non-Catholic Cemeteries Act*, R.S.Q., c. C-17

Saskatchewan: *Cemeteries Act, 1999*, S.S. 1999, c. C-4.01

Yukon: *Cemeteries and Burial Sites Act*, R.S.Y. 2002, c. 25

Public Access to Cemetery Grounds

Burial plots in cemeteries are not generally owned by those whose deceased family members are buried there; nor are burial plots owned by those who plan to be buried in them. In "buying" a burial plot, we actually contract for "interment rights" — a particular use. The land actually remains in the ownership of the cemetery.

As provided in the Ontario legislation, "'interment rights' includes the right to require or direct the interment of human remains in a lot" and "'interment rights holder' means a person with interment rights with respect to a lot." In turn, the *Cemeteries Act*, in the same section, defines a "lot" as "an area of land in a cemetery containing, or set aside to contain, human remains and includes a tomb, crypt, or compartment in a mausoleum and a niche or compartment in a columbarium."[6] Even being an interment rights holder (or "owner") of a burial plot gives a person only very limited rights within that cemetery: the right to inter a person (or be interred) in that plot according to the rules of that cemetery and the right to place a marker on that plot. According to the *Cemeteries Act*:

> s. 23(4) An interment rights holder or the personal representative of the holder has the right to inter any human remains in a lot or other facility approved under this Act in accordance with the bylaws governing the facility.
>
> s. 23(5) An interment rights holder or the personal representative of the holder may erect a commemorative marker on a lot or other receptacle for human remains if the erection of the marker is not in contravention of the bylaws governing the facility.

Even the concept of a "marker" is defined in the *Cemeteries Act*, in s.1, as "any monument, tombstone, plaque, headstone, cornerstone, or other structure or ornament affixed to or intended to be affixed to a burial lot, mausoleum crypt, columbarium niche or other structure or place intended for the deposit of human remains."

After the burial has taken place or the marker has been placed, the Ontario legislation provides for access by the plot "owner" and the relatives of any person buried in a plot for the purpose of decorating the lot: "s. 23(7) An interment rights holder and the relatives of any person whose remains are interred in a cemetery have the right to decorate the appropriate lot *if the decoration is not in contravention of the bylaws governing the facility*." [emphasis added]

It must be noted that this right of access is limited in two ways: first, the person must be either the "owner" of a plot in the cemetery or a relative of a person buried in the plot in order to have access to it under this provision and, second, the access is guaranteed only for the purposes of decorating the plot in accordance with the rules of the cemetery — not for genealogical purposes of information gathering *per se*. The provisions of the new Ontario *Funeral, Burial and Cremation Services Act, 2002*, s. 48 are essentially the same.

While there are provisions in the Ontario legislation for access to cemeteries, members of the public only have a qualified right of access to graves in Ontario cemeteries: "s. 23(6) Every person has the right to reasonable access to a lot at any time *except as prohibited by the by-laws governing the facility*." [emphasis added] This provision is substantially reproduced in the new *Funeral, Burial and Cremation Services Act, 2002*, as s. 5(3)(c).

This means that under the Ontario law "reasonable access" can be limited by cemetery bylaws. Indeed, a number of the provisions of the *Cemeteries Act* are limited by a reference to the bylaws of the cemetery (for example, the right to decorate a burial plot, just discussed).

Although the Ontario *Cemeteries Act* specifically empowers cemetery owners to make bylaws, there are limitations or controls on the bylaws that a cemetery can create. "An owner of a cemetery or crematorium may make by-laws affecting the operation of the cemetery or crematorium."[7] The legislation states that these bylaws will not be effective until filed with and approved by "the Registrar."[8] Another subsection provides for notice: "An owner filing a by-law shall give such notice as is prescribed to such classes of persons as are prescribed."[9] Under the new *Funeral, Burial and Cremation Services Act, 2002*, if and when proclaimed in force, regulations may be made requiring that cemetery bylaws be approved by the Registrar[10] and regulations may be put in place to establish the criteria that the Registrar shall use for this approval process.[11] The current legislation, the *Cemeteries Act*, also provides direction to the Registrar about approving the submitted bylaws:

> A by-law filed with the Registrar under this section shall be approved by the Registrar unless the approval is not in the public interest or the effect of the by-law is to give the owner an unreasonable or unfair competitive advantage over another supplier of cemetery services or supplies.[12]

Thus the law requires the Registrar to assume that a proposed bylaw concerning access to a cemetery should be approved unless it is not in the public interest (since it is hard to imagine a situation in which a bylaw about accessing a cemetery could "give the owner an unreasonable or unfair competitive advantage over another supplier of cemetery services or supplies").

This, in turn, begs the question about what is in the public interest in terms of access to cemeteries. There is no further guidance in the *Cemeteries Act* about this notion of the public interest. Furthermore, there are no legal decisions that give any guidance in this area. Thus, although the bylaws of a cemetery have to be approved through a Registrar, there does not appear to be any clear prohibition to stop cemeteries from limiting or prohibiting public access by bylaw.[13]

The "Registrar" in the *Cemeteries Act* is an office that has not been independently set up in the Ontario government. The functions of this "Registrar" have been discharged at various times by various departments of the Ontario government. Several locations for this function are identified in information found on the web: Mount Pleasant Cemetery Bylaws identified its bylaws as approved by the Ontario Ministry of Government Services Cemeteries Regulation Unit, while North Bay Roman Catholic Cemeteries have identified their bylaws as being regulated and approved by the Ministry of Consumer and Commercial Relations (which was the home under the previous Ontario Government of the function of the Registrar). The Ontario Government website notes the administration of cemeteries as falling to the Ministry of Government Services, Cemeteries Section. The office of this Registrar does not itself have a presence on the web (although there is a contact telephone number for the Registrar buried under information concerning obtaining Death Certificates on the Ontario government website).

While it appears that an Ontario cemetery can restrict access, it is very clear that no charge for access can be imposed. Regulation 130/92 (s. 12), "Establishing, operating and closing cemeteries and crematoria" provides "no owner shall require a person, including a person delivering supplies, to pay for access to the cemetery or crematorium."

It would appear that cemeteries in Ontario have very different attitudes toward public access. For example, both Mount Pleasant Cemetery in Toronto[14] and North Bay Roman Catholic Cemeteries[15] specifically provide in their respective bylaws for hours of operation during which public viewing of the cemetery is allowed. The two cemetery companies have different bylaws regarding the terms of public access: North Bay Roman Catholic Cemeteries does not permit visitors under twelve years of age except in the direct charge of a responsible adult[16] whereas Mount Pleasant Group of Cemeteries has no such criterion. On the other hand, Mount Pleasant Group of Cemeteries specifically provides that "photographing, filming, or video-taping of any part of the Cemetery may only take place with the prior approval of the Cemetery"[17] and North Bay Roman Catholic Cemeteries has no such criterion. Both cemetery owners provide that there shall be no dogs or pets in the cemetery.[18]

There is anecdotal evidence that, in recent years, some Ontario cemeteries have limited access to family members only — and some cemeteries have certainly actively limited photographing tombstones.[19]

St. Peter's Cemetery in London published a notice in the *London Free Press* in 2005 asking people who wanted to view the memorial to the late Pope John Paul, located on the cemetery grounds, to contact the cemetery to make arrangements to visit the memorial.

Anecdotally, based on experiences of genealogists attempting to explore graveyards in Ontario in the past year or two, it appears that there have been situations where cemeteries have completely restricted public access to graves. This evidence was confirmed through consultation with a Compliance Officer in the Ministry of Government Services Cemeteries Branch who confirmed that there are old cemeteries in Ontario, with no known living relatives of the deceased actively maintaining an interest in the graves, which have been closed to the public in the interests of security and maintaining the integrity of the graves and gravesites. He indicated that the owners of these sites should be willing to provide access (reasonably, in daylight hours, where advance requests are made) to genealogists. He also indicated that where graveyards are surrounded by private property not owned by the graveyard owners there is a case to be made for restricting public access to the graveyard because of trespass to the surrounding properties. Finally, he distinguished "public" access for purposes of genealogy, with which he has considerable sympathy, from "public" access to cemeteries for other purposes, such as providing access via the cemetery property to surrounding property for a purpose unconnected with the cemetery or its purposes.

The attitude toward provision of access to cemeteries in other provinces differs from that found in the Ontario laws. In Saskatchewan, the right of public access is unrestricted: "An owner shall provide reasonable access to the public for visitation to any lot in the cemetery." *Cemeteries Act*, Statutes of Saskatchewan, 1999, c. c-4.01, as amended, s. 53(2).[20] British Columbia's recent *Cremation, Interment and Funeral Services Act*, Statutes of British Columbia 2004, c. 35,[21] also assumes a right of access, but only during certain hours:

> s. 9(1) Unless the operator of a place of interment grants prior approval to a person, the person must not enter or remain on land that the person knows or ought to know is a place of interment during a period that is outside of
> (a) the visiting hours, as posted on a sign at the place of interment; or
> (b) the period from 8:00 a.m. to 8:00 p.m., if visiting hours are not posted at the place of interment.

Public Access to the Information Contained in Cemeteries

Up to this point, we have been concentrating on gaining physical access to a cemetery — and have established that *family members* of those buried in a particular cemetery and *those who "own" plots* in that cemetery have rights of access, at least to a particular plot in the cemetery. *Members of the public* in Ontario have rights of reasonable access to cemeteries subject to the ability of a cemetery to prohibit access by bylaw, whereas in Saskatchewan and British Columbia the public's right to reasonable access is explicitly stated. The cemeteries statutes in provinces other than Ontario, British Columbia, and Saskatchewan are silent in this regard.[22] Any Ontario bylaw prohibiting access would have to be approved by the Registrar, who would only be able to refuse to approve such a bylaw if it were not in the public interest. It is nowhere established that providing public access to cemeteries is necessarily in the public interest, so it is possible that a cemetery in Ontario could create a bylaw restricting access. In jurisdictions other than Ontario, Saskatchewan, and British Columbia, it appears that cemeteries would be able to restrict access as they see fit. Assuming, however, that an individual does gain physical access to a cemetery in Canada, are there any legal controls on the use of information that she or he may find within the boundaries of the cemetery?

The City of Niagara Falls, on its website, declares:

> **Privacy Act**
>
> The Ontario Cemeteries Act (1990) states that Cemeteries may only provide the public with the name of the deceased, the date of interment, and the location where they are interred within a cemetery, as well as the name of the Rights Holder of the plot. In keeping with this legislation the City of Niagara Falls Cemetery Services do not record the birth date and death date of the deceased in our Genealogical Search information.[23]

In fact, the Regulations to the Ontario *Cemeteries Act* do make provision for publicly accessible information:[24]

s. 38 (1) The owner shall make available for inspection without charge a public register containing the following information:

1. The name and address of each interment rights holder and the location of the lot to which the rights pertain.

2. The name and address of each original purchaser of interment rights that have been transferred to another person and the date on which the rights were transferred.

3. The name of each person whose remains are interred in the cemetery, the location of the lot in which the remains are interred and the date on which the remains were interred.

4. The name of each person whose remains were cremated in the crematorium, if any, and the date on which the remains were cremated.

5. The particulars of each disinterment of remains, including the name of the person who requested the disinterment, the date on which the remains were disinterred and the location in which the remains were reinterred.

6. The particulars required under section 22. O. Reg. 130/92, s. 38(1). [If money from the Care and Maintenance Fund has been spent on stabilizing or restoring a marker or site, the owner of the cemetery shall record the particulars of the work done and money spent and make the information available for inspection.]

s. 38 (2) The information shall be set out in the public register within five days after the applicable event takes place or after the owner becomes

aware of the information, as the case may be. O.
Reg. 130/92, s. 38(2).

These regulations set out the minimum information that an
Ontario cemetery *must* make publicly available — they do not,
as Niagara Falls seems to have interpreted them, prohibit the
provision of other information — and the information to be
provided is more fulsome than Niagara Falls seems to think. The
Ontario *Cemeteries Act* and its Regulations actually do the opposite
of limiting the information available from accessing a cemetery.
There are, however, two possible areas of legislation that could pose
restrictions: personal data protection legislation and copyright.

The Effect of Personal Data Protection
Legislation on Cemeteries

The particular personal data protection statute that may govern
a particular cemetery in Ontario (or in any other Canadian
jurisdiction) will depend upon the ownership of the cemetery, but
data protection legislation in Canada applies to the records held
by organizations including cemeteries. There is no apparent reason
why the tombstones, monuments, and markers in cemeteries would
not be considered "records." Under the Municipal Freedom of
Information and Protection of Privacy Act in Ontario (MFIPPA),
records are defined as "any record of information however recorded
…."[25] But it should be noted that none of the cemeteries investigated
during the course of my research appeared to explicitly consider
the possibility, when the cemeteries have created and published
their "privacy" statements and policies, that the tombstones, markers,
and monuments in their cemeteries are governed by personal data
protection legislation. It is apparent in these policies and statements

that the cemeteries are considering their personal data protection obligations and responsibilities only in terms of the administrative information generated by their organizations, not in terms of the information contained in the graveyards, mausoleums, and cemeteries themselves. There appear to have been no complaints made to the Information and Privacy Commissioner of Ontario or the federal Privacy Commissioner about the treatment of personal data in cemeteries and so there is no definitive interpretation of the scope of personal data protection in relation to cemeteries.

If a cemetery in Ontario is municipally owned and operated, the applicable personal data protection legislation would be the MFIPPA,[26] but this act applies only to municipalities and other designated bodies.[27] Cemeteries are not specifically mentioned as designated bodies. But, if a cemetery were operated as a department or unit of the municipality, it would be governed by MFIPPA. If, however, cemeteries are operated as independent organizations, although wholly owned by the municipality, they would not be subject to MFIPPA[28] — but could be subject to the same legislation as other commercially operated cemeteries — PIPEDA, discussed later in this chapter.

Even where owned and operated directly by the municipality, the effect of MFIPPA upon the operations of a cemetery may not be dramatic. Under the *Cemeteries Act*, access to information that the cemetery is required to make publicly accessible will be unaffected by MFIPPA. The privacy provisions of MFIPPA, under s. 27, do "not apply to personal information that is maintained for the purpose of creating a record that is available to the general public." Moreover, although the personal data protection provisions of MFIPPA apply to information about an identifiable individual until 30 years after that person's death,[29] the statute does not provide for a way to make a complaint on behalf of a deceased person during that 30-year period. MFIPPA, s. 54, provides that "Any right or power conferred on an individual by this Act may be exercised, if the individual is deceased, by the individual's personal representative [but only] if exercise of the right or power relates to the administration of the individual's estate." It is puzzling to understand, from a legal perspective, exactly why the City of Niagara Falls, for example, explicitly refuses to provide either the birth date or the death date of the deceased in its Genealogical Search Information.

The problem for a municipal cemetery governed by MFIPPA would appear to lie, therefore, mostly with information relating to living individuals that the cemetery would not otherwise be required to make public under the *Cemeteries Act*. The only instance of information about live individuals that visitors might glean from a mausoleum or graveyard would appear to be information about surviving spouses that is sometimes shown on tombstones or markers. Even though it might be thought that by placing information on a tombstone, families intended it to be public, the provisions of the personal data protection legislation will apply if the information is more than is required to be made public under the *Cemeteries Act*.

Municipal cemeteries falling within the purview of MFIPPA would be subject not only to the personal data protection elements of that legislation but also to the access to government-held information aspects of the legislation. Because of this, an individual who wanted any information from those cemeteries, and was denied it, could proceed under MFIPPA for a review of that refusal and ultimately take those proceedings first to the Ontario Information and Privacy Commissioner's Office and then through to the Ontario courts, if necessary. This would clarify, in those situations, the balance to be struck by municipal cemeteries between their obligations to protect personal privacy and their duties to be accessible to the public.

If a cemetery is owned and operated on a commercial basis by a private or religious organization in Ontario, the relevant personal data protection legislation under which it would have to operate is the federal *Personal Information Protection and Electronic Documents Act* (PIPEDA). Cemeteries owned by a municipality, but not part of it, should also be interpreted as commercial entities governed by PIPEDA.

PIPEDA came into full force and effect 1 January 2004. Many of the cemeteries investigated during preparation for this book explicitly acknowledge the application of this legislation to their businesses in their published privacy policies and statements, but they do not discuss the legislation in the context of the information in their cemeteries and mausoleums — the monuments and markers — only in the context of their business information — their contracts and accounting and so on.

Again, as in cemeteries governed by MFIPPA, there is much information in cemeteries governed by PIPEDA that can be freely accessed by members of the public because PIPEDA does not apply. PIPEDA applies to information in records made in the last 100 years, or to information about living individuals and those who have died within the past 20 years — whichever is earlier. This means that information on individuals who died over 20 years ago is freely available even though 100 years have not yet passed since the creation of the monument, marker, or inscription and, vice versa, information on those who are living or have died within the past 20 years is publicly available if the records containing that information are more than 100 years old.[30] PIPEDA, like MFIPPA, only applies to information that the cemetery is not otherwise required to disclose because of other laws, such as the *Cemeteries Act*.[31] Again, as in the case of MFIPPA, there is no provision for access to information about an individual by anyone after that individual's death and no specified mechanism through which anyone can bring a complaint on behalf of the deceased. Clause 4.9 of Schedule 1 to PIPEDA provides for the principle that an individual must be able to access her or his own personal data held by businesses covered by PIPEDA — but there is no provision for access to the information about that individual after death in either the Schedule or the Act itself (see s.8).

Although the PIPEDA complaints system is obscure in the case of deceased persons, privately owned cemeteries are still required to provide personal data protection for the deceased individuals and any living persons whose information is held by them for as long as that protection is required under the statute (until 20 years after death or the record is 100 years old, whichever is the earlier). Moreover, since PIPEDA is only about personal data protection and not about public access, there is no legislated right of public access to information held by private cemetery organizations that compares with the access aspect of the legislation governing public sector institutions. There is therefore no incentive for Ontario's privately owned cemeteries to go beyond the requirements of the *Cemeteries Act* in providing information to the public or permitting members of the public to access that information. If private cemeteries want to err on the side of caution or ease of management, it would seem that they can limit access to information from cemeteries to that which is strictly required under the *Cemeteries Act*. The situation would be similar with respect to privately owned cemeteries in other Canadian jurisdictions.

Copyright Interests in Cemeteries

Returning to the question of areas of law that may affect the ability of members of the public to use information gleaned from access to cemeteries, there is the concern about copyright. More will be said about copyright in the next chapter. This discussion is limited to copyright interests involved in the artifacts of the cemeteries themselves: the tombstones, markers, carvings, and inscriptions. When you take a photograph in a cemetery for yourself, you, as the photographer, will have copyright in that photograph. More will be said about the copyright interests in photographs in the next chapter. Here the discussion will be limited to the question of copyright interests in the elements of the cemetery itself: the tombstones, markers, inscriptions, and carvings.

In past centuries, although copyright law existed, the owners and managers of cemeteries were probably not too concerned about people violating copyright by making reproductions of tombstones. First, the owners of the cemeteries are not normally the holders of copyright in any of the tombstones in their cemeteries and would not therefore likely be involved in any copyright infringement lawsuit about, for example, either sketches done reproducing elements from the memorials in the cemetery or copies made of certain designs of tombstones. Such lawsuits would typically be brought by the sketch artist or monument company connected with a specific grave marker. Second, photography, which has made the copying of tombstones and other elements of the cemetery easy and quick, was not introduced popularly until after the first quarter of the twentieth century, and much of the photography even then was for personal use. If a given photograph were taken and then kept private in the photographer's personal collection, the owner of the copyright in the tombstone or marker that was in the photograph would probably never be aware that the photograph existed, much less be concerned about the copyright implications of the photograph. Since the end of the twentieth century, however, with the burgeoning interest in genealogical research and the growth of the Internet, mass distribution of photographs of tombstones and other elements from cemeteries has increased significantly. These changing conditions have created concerns about copyright infringements.

Certainly not all tombstones, markers, and monuments in a cemetery will be the subject of copyright. Copyright law requires that the **work** in issue be an original one at the time of creation to attract copyright protection.[32] Even if a work was original at the time of its creation, copyright in a work expires after the lifetime of the author or artist plus 50 years from the beginning of the calendar year after the death of the author or artist.[33] Thus the existence of copyright interests in elements of the cemetery does not in any way depend upon the persons buried there or the "owners" of the burial plots. Nor does it depend upon the owners of the cemetery. Any copyright interests involved will be originally those of the creators of the stones, markers, and monuments, or their employers (monument companies).

Thus, the stones, markers, and monuments, as well as sculptures and carvings and so on within the cemetery, can constitute artistic works protected by copyright. As well, the inscriptions on stones, monuments, and markers can constitute literary works protected by copyright, within the limited period of copyright protection — but, again, only if the expressions that are the inscriptions were original when created. The information contained in an inscription, by itself, is just data and not protected by copyright. Only if the information is expressed in an original way does it gain copyright protection. Thus the names and birth and death dates of individuals on a tombstone would not normally attract copyright.

In the 1957 Ontario case of *Kilvington Brothers Ltd. v. Goldberg*,[34] the court specifically decided that a drawing carved onto a tombstone could attract copyright protection. But if the monuments and inscriptions are centuries old, no copyright will remain in them. Even if the monuments and inscriptions are more recent, if they are in an absolutely standard, common form, they will not meet the copyright test of originality and therefore do not have any copyright protection. The judge in the *Kilvington* case put it this way:

> The test is whether this design is original in the sense that it is the original expression of thought of its originator, that it originated from him and that he did not copy it. Ridsdale says that it comes from his own mind and was not a copy of any existing tombstone … this work was the independent creation of Ridsdale. He did not copy it from any source. It embodied features that were common knowledge in the business, but it was more than an automatic or mechanical arrangement of these features. Ridsdale can draw and he did produce out of his own mind and with his own skill an independent work. My conclusion is that copyright exists in the work.

If the tombstone is recent enough and the form of it meets the test of originality, it will be in copyright. Taking a photograph of that tombstone is making a reproduction of that tombstone. Reproduction is a right reserved under the *Copyright Act* for the holder of the copyright.[35] Publishing a photograph of a tombstone that is in copyright in a book or pamphlet or on the Internet would be an infringement of the rights of the copyright holder in that tombstone.[36] On the other hand, however, a genealogist who took a photograph of a tombstone that was a work protected by copyright only in order to further her or his *own* study of genealogy would be protected from a copyright infringement lawsuit, if the copyright holder sued, because of the "fair dealing" provisions of the *Copyright Act* that give users certain rights.[37] Anyone in the process of genealogical research who takes a photograph of a tombstone, whether or not that research is undertaken for profit, would be protected under the fair dealing provisions of the Act. A person who took a photograph of a tombstone to facilitate someone else's genealogical research or study, at that second person's request (acting as agent of the second person), would also be protected by the user's right to fair dealing. The fair dealing provision of the *Copyright Act* would not operate to protect the person in our second scenario if he or she then published that photograph of the tombstone in a book or pamphlet or on the Internet or otherwise without the permission of the tombstone copyright holder.[36] Thus, if a tombstone has attracted copyright protection, then it may still be legal to take a photograph of it, as part of genealogical research, but it would not be permissible to publish that photograph or further disseminate it on the web, for example, without the permission of the copyright holder.

Cemeteries As Information Sources

It is axiomatic that cemeteries function as important information sources for genealogists, as acknowledged by the fact that the Ontario government website links to the Ontario Genealogical Society's microfilms of cemeteries in Ontario.[37] It would appear that there is no clear law in Ontario guaranteeing public access to cemeteries. On the other hand, cemeteries in Ontario do not generally seem to be prohibiting public access, despite the existence of some personal data in cemeteries (for example, on markers and graves) that could be interpreted as coming within the purview of legislated personal data protection. Certainly not all the personal information on markers and graves falls within personal data protection legislation since much of the information is about those who are long dead and other information matches what is required to be published under the *Cemeteries Act*. Ontario cemeteries that are so old that they are not being operated for burying, where the tombstones are all more than 100 years old and where all the information on all the tombstones relates only to people who have been dead for at least 30 years do not involve any interest that is regulated under personal data protection legislation and need only comply with the *Cemeteries Act* — but still need not necessarily provide public access.

Although it has not happened yet, it would appear likely that the scope of personal data protection in Ontario cemeteries will be tested first in the context of municipal cemeteries governed by MFIPPA where personal data protection provisions must be balanced by the statutory right of access to information given to members of the public. Any member of the public could challenge an attempt by a municipal cemetery governed by MFIPPA to limit access to information in a cemetery. Such a challenge would then establish the parameters of personal data protection in the context of cemeteries. Once the requirements to make certain information publicly available under the *Cemeteries Act* (which apply to both municipal and private cemeteries) have been met, there is no incentive or legal requirement for *private* cemeteries governed by the federal PIPEDA legislation to make more information available or accessible — and there is less probability of litigation under this regime, which has no public access component.

Once genealogists have gained access to cemeteries in Ontario and the information that they contain, as discussed, it is important to remember that the ability to use the information gained can be limited by copyright interests. Once again, these limitations will not apply to all artistic and literary works located in cemeteries, but only to those inscriptions, carvings, sculptures, and decorations that were original at the time of their creation and whose creators are either still living or dead within the past 50 years. Even where copyright interests exist, genealogists do have the right to reproduce the monuments and inscriptions and make other uses of them that are consistent with the genealogists' users' rights provided for in the fair dealing provisions and other exceptions to the rights of copyright holders under the *Copyright Act*. This includes using copies of inscriptions, sketches, or photos of the cemetery's monuments and markers for private study and paid or unpaid genealogical researches, either on one's own or as specifically requested by another. These permitted uses fall short of allowing genealogists to publish copies of copyrighted works (in brochures, books, and newsletters, or on the Internet) without getting permission from the holders of the copyright interests in the markers, monuments, inscriptions, or engravings that are the subject of copyright at the time that publication is being contemplated.

The Canadian provinces differ in their attitudes toward the public accessibility to graveyards. For example, in Ontario, certain information must be made available to the public in the records of the cemetery, but access to any cemetery is not guaranteed to people who do not have relatives in the graveyard. Even if you do have a relative in the graveyard, the terms of the purchase of a plot only guarantee access to that plot and not to the whole cemetery in terms of visitation rights to other plots. The ownership of graveyards varies and those that are privately owned now fall under either PIPEDA or provincial private sector personal data protection statutes (or both) and this will make those cemetery owners increasingly conservative in providing access or information about those buried within (particularly where information about the living or the more recently deceased is involved). Finally, other areas of law, besides cemetery and personal data protection regulation are involved if you are thinking about reproducing or publishing exact images taken from cemeteries.

CHAPTER 4

Copyright in Genealogy

One question frequently asked by genealogists is whether they can prevent another person from publishing "their" genealogies. As we have seen in previous chapters, apart from information about the genealogist her- or himself, the information contained in a genealogy is generally considered to be the personally identifiable information of persons other than the genealogist and, therefore, as information *per se*, genealogists have little opportunity to control subsequent uses once "their" genealogies leave their hands — certainly not through the personal data protection statutes. This is because if the genealogist is doing genealogy strictly in a private capacity, as a hobby, the information with which she or he is working will not fall within the purview of personal data protection legislation. If the genealogist is a person working at genealogy as a paid undertaking in Canada, personal data protection legislation may well apply to the research. However, the enforcement of rights under the personal data protection regimes lies with the person who is the subject of the information or with those administering the regime, not with other individuals such as the person who originally compiled the genealogy. Thus personal data protection legislation does not give *the genealogist* any control over subsequent uses of her or his genealogy once distributed to others.

Genealogists frequently argue, however, that the amount of labour expended in collecting and organizing information about a family should entitle them to control the subsequent uses of the genealogy by others. Copyright is the area of law that is most often considered to provide this kind of control. Because of international treaties to which Canada is a party, all information being used in Canada, no matter where its source, is treated as governed by the Canadian *Copyright Act*.

In this chapter, we will consider whether (and, if so, to what extent) copyright interacts with genealogy.

A genealogist can be involved with copyright in two ways:

1. Copyright may affect what a genealogist can do with information that comes into her or his hands during research; and
2. Copyright may give a genealogist certain controls over the product she or he creates from her or his research.

In either case, the first question is whether the information involved qualifies as a "work" or "other subject matter" as defined by the Canadian *Copyright Act*.

How Can You Tell Whether the Information Involved Is a "Work" in Copyright?

The *Copyright Act* says that "every original literary, dramatic, musical or artistic work" is governed under the *Copyright Act* as soon as it is created. Every original sound recording, broadcast, or performer's performance (the "other subject matter") is also governed under the *Copyright Act* as soon as recorded, broadcast, or performed. Genealogists appear to use and create any of the three kinds of "other subject matter" very, very infrequently. Therefore this chapter will concentrate on "works" under the *Copyright Act*. Both works and other subject matter are considered to be expressions of ideas or facts and, if they are original, are entitled to copyright protection for a certain length of time.

A key word here is "original." If something is not an original creation, then it never becomes subject to the *Copyright Act*. And, if it never becomes subject to the *Copyright Act*, it can freely circulate in society. Copyright has always been intended to permit idea and facts to circulate freely while at the same time giving some control over certain uses of original expressions to copyright holders and creators for a period of years.

Thus, logically, every piece of information that is embodied in a work that is older than the longest term of copyright in Canada must be freely available to any genealogist working in Canada to use, copy, post on the Internet or otherwise, subject, of course, to any other constraints imposed by other areas of law such as personal data protection legislation or libel. The same also holds true for any piece of information that is embodied in an expression that is not original, whatever the age of the expression. The chapter on cemeteries pointed out that merely reproducing the names and birth and death dates inscribed on a tombstone, without actually photographing or drawing the stone, would normally not have any consequence under copyright law because there would be no originallity in the expression of the information.

What Sources of Information Used by Genealogists Tend Not to Be "Original"?

"Literary works" protected by copyright are not just those works that are works of literary merit, as English majors would use the term. In copyright terms, "literary" really just means "text." Thus, any piece of text that is original will be considered a "literary work" and entitled to copyright.

Obituaries and death notices are sources frequently used for genealogy and are either entirely or mostly textual. Are they literary works protected by copyright? Actually, because death notices routinely follow a standard formula, they generally do not display enough originality to attract copyright protection. Obituaries, being often more extensive and detailed, have greater possibilities for achieving the level of orginality required to be protected in copyright but, to the extent that an obituary contains formulaic or standard elements, the likelihood of its being original enough to attract copyright protection is reduced.

Interestingly, while there appear to be no reported legal decisions in Canada involving copyright in obituaries, there are reports of litigation involving alleged libels in obituaries! (This is the case even though a libel lawsuit cannot be brought for defamation of a dead person.)[1]

Forms that have not changed for several centuries could not be considered to be original. Any copyright that had ever existed in them would have long since expired. For example, a church might be using forms that were established in the early 1800s to record information about recent parishioners. In such cases, it would have been the form itself, and not the facts contained in the form, that would have originally attracted copyright protection — but such an old form, even if it contains information inserted just yesterday, would no longer be subject to copyright and will be free for the genealogist to use in any way.

Photographs are "artistic" works under the *Copyright Act* and will usually be considered to be original works and thus will be in copyright as long as the period of protection for them has not expired. The copyright in a photograph will exist whether or not a photograph of a tombstone is of identifiable people or of tombstones or of anything else. The several copyrights reflected in the photograph will, at least initially, be owned by different people. Further reproduction of the photograph would require permission of each of the copyright holders with a copyright interest: the photographer, stonemason, and author of, for example, the poem engraved on it.

When Does the Copyright in an Original "Work" Expire?

Even if there is enough originality in an expression of creativity to be protected in copyright, the copyright will expire after a time. How long the copyright lasts is covered by the *Copyright Act*.

Generally, the normal period of protection for works in copyright is the life of the author plus 50 years. Actually, to be precise, all these time limits run from the end of calendar years, so, for example: "the life of the author, the remainder of the calendar year in which the author dies, and a period of fifty years following the end of that calendar year" but, for ease and economy of expression in this chapter, the periods will just be referred to in years. Life of the author plus 50 years will be referred to in this chapter as the "normal" period of copyright. It must be noted that the period of protection is calculated from the life of the author even if he or she is not the first or the eventual *owner* of a particular copyright interest in the work.

Where a work's author is unknown, the copyright runs for the shorter of 50 years following publication of the work or 75 years after the work was first created. The work's author is thought to be either anonymous or known by a pseudonym. If the actual author becomes generally known, the period of protection will run for the life of the author plus 50 years. Where there are multiple authors of a work, the period of copyright runs 50 years from the death of the last surviving author.

There are, however, three areas where the *Copyright Act* provides different terms of copyright that are particularly interesting to those engaged in genealogy.

First, if a provincial or federal government department or agency holds copyright in a work, the period of copyright belongs to the government, unless there was a special arrangement made with the author, and will run only for 50 years following the work's preparation or publication. The *Copyright Act* says, "where any work is, or has been, prepared or published by or under the direction or control of Her Majesty or any government department." This does not apply to works involving municipal governments or agencies: there the copyright interests last for the normal period of time. (In this, Canada differs dramatically from the copyright situation in the United States. Under American copyright legislation, the American federal government cannot hold copyright in anything created by it — and many states have made similar provisions for works created by them.) It should also be noted that some writers on copyright matters suggest that, because s. 12 of the Canadian *Copyright Act* mentions "publication" as a trigger for the period of protection of 50 years in federal and provincial government materials (known as "Crown copyright"), unpublished material created by the Crown in Canada is perpetually in copyright. However, the stronger interpretation, given here, is that the effect of s.12 is merely to shorten the normal term of protection. This position relies on the fact that s.6 of the *Copyright Act* creates the "normal" term: s. 5 declares that copyright shall exist "for the term hereinafter mentioned in every original literary, dramatic, musical and artistic work …"; and s. 12 itself speaks of both "published by or under the direction or control of Her Majesty" *and* "prepared … by or under the direction or control of Her Majesty," which must mean that being published is not the determining factor. There are as yet no court decisions that explicitly endorse either interpretation.

Second, there is a slightly complicated situation currently in Canada when an author dies before a literary, dramatic, or musical work (or an engraving) is published, performed in public, or communicated to the public by telecommunication. Note that this complexity in the *Copyright Act* does not occur with respect to artistic works other than engravings. Thus, for example, it does not occur in the case of photographs. This complication will be of interest to genealogists working with unpublished letters or diaries or other private written records (but not photographs). Generally, the Canadian government is moving the law toward the position that these works have the normal term of copyright and has done so in a series of steps, depending upon the date of death of the author. In the first case, all works *whose authors died before 1949*, whether or not the works were published, performed, or communicated before the death of the author, are now out of copyright. In the second case, where *the author died between 1949 and the end of 1998*, and the works had not been published, performed, or communicated before the death of their author, the works still remain in copyright because the *Copyright Act* says such works remain in copyright for 50 years from the date of the amendment in 1998 (*these copyright interests will end 31 December 2048*) — whereas if a work was published, communicated publicly, or performed during the author's lifetime, and the author died between 1948 and 1998, copyright expires 50 years later, thus, between 1998 and 2048. In the third case, all works existing now where *the author has died or will die after 31 December 1998*, whether or not their works have been or will be published before their deaths, are in copyright for the normal period.

The other area of unusual terms of copyright is photographs. This is an area where the Canadian government has made a number of changes to the *Copyright Act*, most recently in 1997. The law at this moment is quite technical and depends upon who the owner of the negative is (or the photograph itself, where there is no negative involved in the process) at the time the photograph is created. If the owner of the negative is a large corporation, then the term of copyright will be 50 years from its making; but if it is an individual person or a "small company," the copyright will be the normal term. And, in the small corporate situation, the "life" will be the life of the majority shareholder. On the other hand, in the case of commissioned photographs, the *owner* of the photograph will be the commissioning party, not the individual taking the photograph or her or his employer, and this will usually leave the copyright in photographs of family members, for example, with the normal length of copyright.

Thus, although it can be difficult at times to discern which term of copyright applies to a particular work in hand, there is a great deal of material of interest to genealogists that is free to them to consult, copy, publish, or make any use they like of, without any concern about copyright.

As of 2009 it would probably be virtually risk-free for a genealogist to treat all of the following as freely available without concern for copyright interests:

1. All material that did not, at the time of creation, possess enough originality to be included as "work" under the *Copyright Act*.

2. All materials created before 1899. I arrive at this by using the same Statistics Canada evidence of life expectancy used by the Ontario Information and Privacy Commissioner's Office for calculating periods of personal data protection (discussed in Chapter 1), 60 years, and adding the 50 year period of copyright protection after death, for a total possible period of copyright of 110 years. If a person lived longer than the expected 60 years, this date of 1899 for a work is still safe because it is unlikely that anyone created a work still of interest today before turning 20 years old.

3. Any photographs taken before 1959 that the genealogist knows were taken originally by someone on the staff at a large company and were not commissioned by someone else.

4. Any material that the genealogist knows was originally prepared or published by the federal government or government agency or any provincial government or government agency before 1959.

5. Any material that was unpublished prior to the death of the author, where the author died before 1949.

If a Work Is in Copyright, How Can a Genealogist Use It Without Seeking Permission or Paying for the Use?

Even if a work is in copyright, there are certain "users' rights"[2] created by the Canadian *Copyright Act* that permit a genealogist to make use of copyright material without seeking permission or paying anything. Probably the most relevant set of rights of interest to genealogists is known as "fair dealing." Under these sections of the *Copyright Act*, an individual can use copyrighted material for research or private study. (Fair dealing also includes rights to use materials for criticism, review, and news reporting, if the source is given and, if given in the source, the author of a work is mentioned.) The research does not have to be personal research — it can be research being done as part of a business: thus, both genealogists engaged in genealogy as a hobby and those engaged in it as a profession can use any copyrighted material in any way they see fit in connection with their research, without permission from anyone and without paying royalties to anyone. It is also probably possible for a genealogist to make copies for another person who is involved in research or private study (acting as their agent, in effect) — but probably not possible for the genealogist to make multiple copies at once for groups of people.[3]

The American version of "fair dealing" is known as "fair use" — but it is different from the Canadian enactment. In addition to the provisions for fair dealing, the Canadian *Copyright Act* contains a number of other sections that create users' rights in copyrighted material (or, as they are also considered, exceptions to the rights of the copyright holders), particularly for most educational institutions, libraries, archives, and museums. There is also one specifically permitting religious, educational, and charitable institutions (for example, church choirs), in furtherance of their religious, educational, or charitable goals, to perform live music or play sound recordings without compensating the copyright holders. Another well-publicized users' right in Canada is the right to private copying, under which copies of music recordings may be made for the private use of a listener.

It is another matter, however, if the genealogist, having used a copyrighted work in research or private study, goes on to make another use of the work, such as publishing it in a book, reproducing it for groups as part of a talk, or posting the work to the Internet. When the second use is made, after the use as part of the research process, that second use would require the permission of the copyright holder — and that copyright holder may wish to charge for that use. If a church, for example, has copyright in a record that a genealogist has copied pursuant to her right to research and if the genealogist wishes to make copies of that record for a whole group as a matter of interest or for any number of family members, the permission of the church must be sought for this new use of the work. This is true even if a genealogist has received a copy of a record pursuant to a request under access legislation or under personal data protection legislation: while the first copy from the institution is given to the requestor as a right and without any copyright concern, any subsequent uses of that record are subject to the copyright holders' rights. The first copy is made without copyright consequence because the *Copyright Act* has a specific exemption for copies made pursuant to access and personal data protection legislation.[4]

What Uses Are Controlled by Those Who Hold Copyright in Works?

First of all, under the Canadian *Copyright Act*, the copyright holder can only exercise rights in connection with the whole or a substantial part of a work in copyright. Again, while substantiality is a concept also involved in the American copyright legislation, the question of substantiality arises in a different context than the point being made here in connection with Canadian copyright law. In Canada, see the language of s. 3 of the *Copyright Act*. So a genealogist publishing only an insubstantial portion of a literary work, such as a portion of a letter, does not need the permission of the copyright holder. One problem with acting upon this ability is that there is no objective test that can be applied in advance in determining what a court may later consider to be a substantial portion of a work. Nevertheless, Canadians have had long experience of quoting from one work in the writing of another without needing to seek copyright permission from the first author.

In addition to being able to make use of insubstantial portions of works without infringing copyright, Canadians now have a defence in the *Copyright Act* that permits them to make an "incidental use" of even the whole of a work by including it "incidentally and not deliberately" in another work or other subject matter. Added in 1997, this defence, in s. 30.7 of the *Copyright Act*, has not yet received any real testing in the courts. Such a situation could arise when, for example, a family portrait is reproduced with appropriate permission from the copyright owner, but it is later noticed that the family was photographed in front of an original painting that is in copyright, and the permission of the artist had not been sought when the photograph was reproduced.

A copyright holder's permission should be sought if the genealogist deliberately uses a substantial part or the whole of a work in copyright (other than for "fair dealing" purposes) and does any of the following:

- Copies the work;
- If the work is unpublished, publishes the work;
- Produces, reproduces, performs, or publishes a translation of the work; or
- Communicates the work to the public by telecommunication.

Copyright holders control other uses of works under the *Copyright Act*, but it seems unlikely that genealogists will be making such uses: perform the work in public; convert a dramatic work into a novel or other non-dramatic work; convert a novel, other non-dramatic work, or artistic work into a dramatic work (by way of performance in public or otherwise); make a sound recording or film of a literary, dramatic, or musical work; reproduce, adapt, and publicly present a work as a film; publicly exhibit artistic works (except maps, plans, and charts) made after 7 June 1988 (except for sale or hire); rent out computer programs or sound recordings of musical works; or authorize any of the acts reserved to copyright holders.

Posting material to the Internet will involve a genealogist in at least one of these uses[5] — and is not included in uses that can conceivably lie within users' rights (for example, research or private study). Therefore, permission to post material to the Internet should be sought where substantial parts of works in copyright are involved.

Copyright holders can enforce their rights under the *Copyright Act* by suing people they believe to be infringing their copyrights. A copyright holder can sue any one or group of genealogists whom they believe are infringers: who to sue is a choice the copyright holder controls.

The copyright holder must prove the infringement to a court. The genealogist is entitled to defend by arguing that:

1. the work in question is not a work in copyright; and/or
2. the person or company suing is not the legal owner of the copyright interest in question; and/or
3. the use of the work was of an insubstantial portion of the work; and/or
4. the use made of the work was not a use that the copyright holder has; and/or

5. the genealogist was exercising a user's right in connection with the use of the copyrighted work.

If the copyright holder succeeds, the court can order the genealogist to stop using the work, including ordering a copyright-infringing work to be withdrawn from circulation and/or the court can order the genealogist to pay a sum of money set by the court (damages) to the copyright holder and/or, finally, the court can require the genealogist to pay some or, in very rare cases, all of the costs the copyright holder incurred in bringing the lawsuit against the genealogist.

The *Copyright Act* also contains criminal sanctions against copyright infringement, with potential penalties that were dramatically increased in 1988. Fines for a summary conviction offence can be up to $25,000 and a court may impose instead, or in addition, a sentence of imprisonment for up to six months. For a more serious conviction, on indictment, a fine of up to $1 million dollars may be imposed, or a court may impose, in addition or instead, a prison sentence of up to five years. It would only be in a very, very rare instance that copyright holders would be able to persuade the attorneys general and the courts in this country that criminal enforcement of copyright in the sort of situations in which genealogists would find themselves is appropriate.

If Permission Is Needed, from Whom Should the Genealogist Seek It?

Under the *Copyright Act*, the original copyright owner is either the personal author or creator of the work or the employer for whom that author or creator was working at the time. There is a special provision where a photograph or portrait was commissioned. In that case, if the portrait or photograph is paid for in full, the ownership of the portrait, the negative, or the photograph lies with the commissioning party, not the photographer. Here again the Canadian law differs from the American. Many photography outlets in Canadian department stores that have head offices in the United States routinely stamp photographs commissioned by customers as belonging to the store. However, under Canadian law, unless the contract between the customer and the store for the taking of the photograph explicitly provides otherwise, the ownership of the copyright in the photo, commissioned and taken in Canada, is, under Canadian law, the customer's.[6] This is, of course, helpful to genealogists because it is often evident from the pose or position of the subjects of a formal photograph that it was commissioned and, if it is still within the period of copyright for the photograph, the subject or subjects or their heirs will be able to give permission for any uses of the photograph by the genealogist where permissions are necessary.

Where the original owner of the copyright is a company, because the company is the employer of the author or creator, the length of copyright of that work will be determined by the lifetime of the employee-author or -creator, plus 50 years; the "lifetime" of the company is not relevant.

Letters provide genealogists with the occasional difficulty. The owner of copyright in a letter is the author of the letter (or, in the case of business correspondence, the employer of the author employee) — never the recipient of the letter.

Under the *Copyright Act*, the first owner of copyright in a work is given worldwide rights in a whole bundle of uses of the work. The *Copyright Act* specifically permits the owner of the copyright to sell or give away each of those rights independent of the others and to "subdivide" each of the rights geographically (the right to sell a book in Japan or in Germany or in Canada or in the United States, etc.) or according to a particular market (for example, marketing a book to children, to teens, or to adults) or otherwise (the rights to the Chinese-language film adaptation of a book, the rights to the Arabic translation of a book, or the Latin). Thus, as a genealogist seeking permission to make a certain specific use of a copyrighted work, the key is to find the current owner of that specific use for that copyrighted work. Since this is a chapter about making use of material in Canada, the use for which the genealogist is seeking permission must be a use in Canada — and thus the copyright holder from whom permission must be sought must be the holder of rights in Canada for the use sought.

The first way to search for such copyright holders may be to consult the list of collective organizations published by the Copyright Board of Canada.[7] In Canada, collectives administer many rights on behalf of rights-holders, including the right to photocopy material. AccessCopyright (formerly known as Cancopy) administers this right for literary works in Canada, except in Quebec. AccessCopyright can also represent works in Quebec in giving permissions because it has a reciprocal agreement with COPIBEC in Quebec (formerly with UNEQ). If a collective in Canada represents a use for which you are seeking permission, that is the sole source for that permission, not the individual rights-holder (unless the rights-holder has chosen not to be part of the collective). A collective will tell you whether it represents the rights-holder you are seeking. Unfortunately, perhaps, from a potential user's point of view, there are certain rights where the Canadian rights-holders have yet to form a collective association and so it is not possible to approach a collective for permission. This is the case still with respect to rights to upload material in copyright to the Internet. Here, you must find the individual rights-holder and approach that person or company directly. It is also the case generally with unpublished material that is in copyright.

A second way to locate a copyright holder in Canada would be to check the Register of Copyrights in Ottawa. Although it is not necessary to register a copyright in Canada to enforce it, it is possible to register some interests in copyright — and many copyright holders do. Thus a search of the Register may be helpful to genealogists trying to locate a copyright holder but will not provide definitive information about the existence of a copyright interest in a work or the ownership of it. See *www.ic.gc. ca/app/opic-cipo/cpyrghts/dsplySrch.do?lang=eng.*

Copyright is a monopoly right, which means that only one person at a time can hold the right to a particular use for the whole country of Canada. Even if it appears that there is a rights-holder (a publisher, for example) in the United States or elsewhere in the world willing to give you permission to use a work more cheaply than the cost quoted to you by a Canadian rights-holder, you must nevertheless deal with the Canadian rights-holder — inevitably it will turn out that the foreign rights-holder was unaware that you were requesting permission for Canada. Whatever the state of their knowledge, unless someone actually holds the rights for Canada, you cannot rely on the permission received, even if it is in writing. No one can sell or give you permissions that they have no right to give. If you choose to "buy" from a person who does not hold valid rights to the use in Canada that you are seeking, and you use the copyrighted material, you will be liable for copyright infringement if the rightful Canadian holder sues you.

There is a provision in the Canadian *Copyright Act* that can be useful in locating copyright owners toward the end of the period of the copyright, for works originally owned by the author her- or himself that have the normal period of protection.[8] Twenty-five years before the copyright expires, no matter what transfers of copyright interests have happened up to that point, all the copyright interests in a work (except a work that has been included in a larger collective work, such as a chapter in a book) will revert to the ownership of the author's heirs. Thus, for the last 25 years of the period of the copyright, if you can find an author's heirs, you can make arrangements for a copyright use with them.

If you believe that a work is in copyright and you have tried unsuccessfully to locate the proper holder of the rights in Canada from whom to seek permission, there is a unique provision under the Canadian *Copyright Act* that will allow you to seek permission from the Copyright Board to make the use that you wish.[9] Unfortunately, it only operates for works that have been published.

What about the Moral Rights in a Work?

The Canadian *Copyright Act* provides for another set of rights that arise upon creation of a work. This is another area where American copyright legislation differs dramatically from the Canadian: the American legislation does not explicitly provide for moral rights at all. Moral rights in Canada last for the same period of time as the other rights in works that have been discussed above — but these works always arise only in the author, whether or not that author is in the employment of another at the time of creation of the work, and these rights always remain with the author or with her or his heirs (they cannot be sold). These rights remain with authors throughout their lifetimes and with their heirs for the 50 years following their deaths, although authors (or their heirs after their deaths) can waive them.

- One of these rights is the right, where reasonable in the circumstances, to be associated with the work as the author chooses — either as anonymous author, by pseudonym, or by name. This right is generally known as the right to paternity.
- Another is known as the right to integrity in the work: the author is entitled to object to the distortion, mutilation, or other modification of the work, to the prejudice of her or his honour or reputation.
- The final Canadian moral right is the right of the author to object to the use of her or his work in association with a product, service, cause, or institution to the prejudice of her or his honour or reputation.

Although it is useful for the genealogist to be aware of these rights of authors and be aware that permission received for certain uses from a copyright holder is not the same as permission from the author with respect to moral rights, it appears unlikely that a genealogist will be involved in uses that involve the author's moral rights.

What about the Genealogist As Author?

When a genealogist has put a great deal of effort into compiling a genealogy, there is a tendency to want to control the future uses of that information. But does a genealogist have a legal right to control the future uses of a genealogy? A genealogist who wants to rely on copyright to control uses by others of her or his genealogies has several hurdles to overcome.

The first hurdle is the question of originality in the creation of the genealogy: genealogical charts follow a uniform structure and the information recorded in them is recorded in predictable and standard ways. Because of this, even though the information in each genealogy is unique, it is factual: the presentation of the genealogy, the work itself, the expression of the information, is not original enough to attract copyright protection. On the other hand, if the genealogical information or research is expressed in the form of stories or essays written by the genealogist, there probably is sufficient originality in those expressions to attract copyright protection.

The second hurdle in modern genealogy is the use of commercial software to create the genealogies. Software is itself classified as a literary work under the *Copyright Act*. Technically, in Canada, computer software, *per se*, cannot be the subject of a patent. Additionally, computer automation of a process can be protected in patent for 20 years if it is novel, unobvious, and useful, and therefore registered in Ottawa as a patent.[10] Genealogical software in Canada is typically licensed by genealogists from commercial companies that hold the copyrights in the software for the genealogy (and, in some cases, patent interests as well). These licences dictate the uses that the genealogist may make of that software and thus dictate what uses the genealogist may make of the genealogies created with the software they have purchased. Somewhat surprisingly, in making presentations to genealogists across Ontario, including to genealogists from other provinces, I have been advised that there is no open source software in use for genealogy.

Similarly, a genealogist using material provided through a website may be required to enter into a licensing agreement with the website operator. Such website operators virtually always include intellectual property provisions in the licensing agreements into which they require users to enter. These legally limit the uses users can make of the information acquired through the website. The following are typical clauses in such agreements:

You [the User genealogist] acknowledge and agree that all Intellectual Property Rights in all material or content supplied as part of the website shall remain at all times vested in Us [the company operating the website]. You are permitted to use this website and the material contained therein only as expressly authorized by Us.

You acknowledge and agree that the material and content contained within the website is made available for your personal, non-commercial use only and that you may (if necessary to make a Purchase) download such material and content on to only one computer hard drive for such purpose. Any other use of the material and content of the website is strictly prohibited. ... You may not create and/or publish your own database that features substantial parts of this website.

This agreement asserts the company's copyright interests in all the material made available on its website. It does not permit a professional genealogist to use this material as only personal, non-commercial uses are permitted. It limits the use of material from the website gathered while "browsing" to one computer — and it doesn't permit any other use of the material without a "Purchase" being made. In the case of the website from which these specific clauses are quoted, the "Purchase," a separate transaction for the User genealogist from the one to which these clauses pertain, would give the User genealogist certain rights to use copyrighted works from the website in certain ways, for certain fees.

Thus, in most situations, not only does the genealogist not have copyright in the genealogies and genealogical information compiled by her or him, but the software companies supplying the genealogical software and the operators of the websites used in the compilation of the genealogy actually can control future uses of the genealogies — even those "authored" by the genealogist himself or herself.

If a Genealogist Publishes a Work Based on Genealogy, Must It Be Deposited in Ottawa?

This last question is a question raised with me by genealogists familiar with the operation of Canada's depository program. Under this program, two copies of certain publications published in Canada must be deposited with Library and Archives Canada and the publication itself will be assigned a unique number, an International Standard Book Number — an ISBN. This program is legislated under the *Library and Archives of Canada Act, 2004* — and continues a longstanding program of the former National Library of Canada. (Since 2004, the National Library and the National Archives in Canada have been combined.) To be required to make this deposit, the genealogical work must meet certain criteria. First, it must be published and made available, with or without charge, in Canada. Material created solely for distribution to members of a genealogical group or a group of friends, for example, would not therefore qualify. Second, there is a class of works that are *not* required to be deposited unless requested in writing by the Librarian and Archivist of Canada.[11] This class of works has traditionally included printed books only manufactured and distributed in Canada and not published under the imprint of a Canadian publisher — this would include genealogical books that are self-published by genealogists or published by genealogical associations in Canada.[12] The class also includes books produced for initial release of fewer than four copies or books circulating only in drafts or as works-in-progress.[13] Finally, it includes "newsletters of local interest, in particular those that are published by associations."[14] Furthermore, where more than four copies but fewer than 100 copies have been produced — or where publication has been done online — only one copy of the publication is required to be deposited, rather than the two copies required if more than 100 are produced. With respect to online publications, no copy is required to be deposited of websites or electronic discussion groups, listservs, bulletin boards, or e-mails unless a request is received from the Librarian and Archivist.

This discussion of copyright completes this canvas of the law that can affect genealogists in Canada in seeking information and passing their findings on to others. As we have seen, the key to its application is the fact that the genealogist is working *in* Canada — not where the information with which the genealogist is working has come from. It can also be seen that the situation of the Canadian genealogist is unique: the laws that affect Canadian genealogists are not the same as the laws affecting genealogists working outside Canada. While all Canadian genealogists experience the same copyright law, with respect to information in cemeteries or personal data protection law, the experience of Canadian genealogists can differ from province to province. Copyright, while important, may not be the barrier for genealogists that its complexity might make it appear at first blush. The ubiquity of commercial software and proprietary websites in genealogy, rather than open source software and open access information sites, may prove much more of a barrier for genealogists when they want to share the products of their genealogical researches than copyright law is in Canada. Personal data protection, especially for professional genealogists, imposes a significant burden (see Chapter 2). Personal data protection may also affect both professional genealogists and those doing genealogy as a hobby in their efforts to access Canadian sources of information (as both Chapters 1 and 2 discuss).

CHAPTER 5

Genealogy and Libel Law

This chapter will provide a basic introduction to what constitutes libel, when a lawsuit may arise, and what defences exist if a claim is made against you.

What Constitutes Libel?

Libel is technically a subsection of what is more generally known in the law as defamation. Strictly speaking, libel only refers to written forms of defamation and spoken forms are known as slander. Colloquially, though, both forms of defamation, which are statements that may have a negative impact on a person's reputation, are commonly referred to as libel. Historically, the written form of defamation, libel, has been treated as more serious than slander, as the written form was considered to be able to be more widely distributed and its existence as a published item has been thought to lend it a more permanent nature than spoken words have.

Not just any publicly available material to which an individual may take offence will be found to be libelous. That would be entirely too difficult to predict, leading any person writing any work to be overly cautious about offending others. In a broad definition, any statement that "lowers [a person] in the esteem of others"[1] can be libellous.

In his book Media Law for Canadian Journalists, *Dean Jobb identifies and explains a list of topics that today, in Canada, are often thought to be particularly sensitive, wherein comments are likely to be considered capable of negatively affecting a person's reputation. These include comments related to such topics as racism, financial problems, deceit or dishonesty, sexual harassment or sexual misconduct, and incompetence.*[2]

If someone decides to sue you for libel, the lawsuit will proceed in two parts. First, the person suing you (the plaintiff) will have to prove three things before the lawsuit can proceed further:

1. That a reasonable person reading the text alleged to be libellous would identify the person suing you as the one to whom reference is being made in the text; and

2. That the alleged libel was actually published, broadcast, or made available to a wider audience than a private communication would be (for example, the libel did not occur as part of a private communication between the plaintiff and you); and

3. That a reasonable person would consider the statements to be harsh or negative enough to negatively affect the plaintiff's reputation.

Because Quebec is a civil law province, its law respecting libel is different. Most notably, in Quebec, libel can be established even if only the creator and the person libelled are aware of the material — the material need not be available to the wider world.[3]

Once the plaintiff has been able to establish that all three of these criteria have been established, you, as a defendant in such a lawsuit, will have an opportunity to establish that the circumstances mean that your conduct was still appropriate in the circumstances.

Both the criteria that the person suing you must prove and those that you must prove have to be established in court on a balance of probabilities, which is the burden of proof in a lawsuit between private individuals. This burden of proof differs from the situation in a criminal lawsuit where the Crown is involved and the burden of proof that the Crown must establish against an accused person is proof beyond a reasonable doubt.[4] It is a peculiarity of lawsuits involving defamation such as libel that the burden of proof upon you, as a defendant establishing circumstances that justify a libel, once that libel has been proven on a balance of probabilities by the plaintiff, requires you to prove those circumstances on a balance of probabilities. In other civil lawsuits, the defendant never has to meet a burden of proof but simply must provide enough evidence to refute the plaintiff's efforts to meet the requirement of proof on a balance of probabilities.

We will look first in more detail at what the plaintiff must establish and then turn in more detail to the circumstances to which you can point in order to defend yourself. The discussion here will be general. Although the common law has long recognized libel and slander, each of the common law jurisdictions in Canada (that is, all the territories and every province except Quebec) has passed a statute that specifically governs the conduct of an action for defamation in that province or territory. Quebec, as a civil law jurisdiction and thus lacking law made purely through judicial decisions, governs defamation entirely through legislation. The federal government is not involved in the law of defamation in Canada. Here are listed all the statutes in Canada that deal with libel.

Statutes Relating to Libel

Alberta: *Defamation Act*, R.S.A. 2000, c. D-7

British Columbia: *Libel and Slander Act*, R.S.B.C. 1996, c. 263

Manitoba: *Defamation Act*, C.C.S.M. c. D-20

New Brunswick: *Defamation Act*, R.S.N.B. 1973, c. D-5

Newfoundland and Labrador: *Defamation Act*, R.S.N.L. 1990, c. D-3

Nova Scotia: *Defamation Act*, R.S.N.S. 1989, c. 122

Nunavut and Northwest Territories: *Defamation Act*, R.S.N.W.T. 1988, c. D-1

Ontario: *Libel and Slander Act*, R.S.O. 1990, c. L.12

Prince Edward Island: *Defamation Act*, R.S.P.E.I. 1988, c. D-5

Quebec: *Civil Code of Québec* [C.C.Q.], S.Q. 1991, c. 64, Article 1457

Saskatchewan: *Libel and Slander Act*, R.S.S. 1978, c. L-14

Yukon: *Defamation Act*, R.S.Y. 2002, c. 52

How can you tell if you have libelled someone?

1. Even if the name of the person suing you does not appear in the publication, if the description or information given is clear enough so that other people would identify this particular individual or identifiable group of individuals, the comment will still be considered to refer to that person or group.

2. Anyone who publishes or republishes a libellous statement can be held responsible for doing so and the person offended, at her or his own option, can sue any or all of those involved in transmitting the information. Even if a person is not the originator of the libel, as long as she or he has somehow assisted in spreading the material by publishing it, she or he may

be held liable for defamation. In the case *Cherneskey v. Armadale Publishers Ltd.*,[5] Cherneskey sued a newspaper for publishing defamatory contents that were part of a reader's opinion letter. The newspaper did not create the material: the writer of the letter did. Nonetheless, Canada's Supreme Court held that the newspaper, by publishing the letter, assisted in its dissemination to the public and was therefore accountable. On the other hand, if you create material that is libellous, but do not yourself make it available to the public (by putting it in a newspaper or on a website, for example), you will not be held responsible for libelling anyone *unless* you consented, or implied that you were consenting, to having that libellous material made available to the public by someone else.

3. Publishing something that is embarrassing to another person is not necessarily libellous. More than embarrassment is required to be proven by the person suing for libel: the person must have a reputation in the community that has been negatively affected by the material that has been published.

How should you defend yourself against claims that you have libelled someone?

Though it may be ill-mannered to "speak ill of the dead," the law in the common-law provinces and territories of Canada does not provide the estate of a deceased person any remedy for libel about that dead person.[6]

On the other hand, material published primarily about a deceased person can have an impact on the reputations of the living and, in these cases, the living persons affected can sue for libel. In 1910, the case of *Barnes v. Carter*,[7] about an obituary, was

> *Quebec appears more open to libel cases against deceased persons. In a lawsuit brought in 1915, a daughter succeeded in a claim that her deceased father was libelled by the suggestion that she was his illegitimate daughter.*[8]

decided by an Ontario court. The deceased's daughter claimed that the obituary inferred that she was the man's illegitimate child and the court agreed that this inference should be considered libellous. However, the court ultimately ruled that the daughter had not met all the requirements to establish her libel claim. In 1995, another case in Ontario was decided involving publication of an obituary. In the 1995 case, *Allen v. Bailey*,[9] the mistress of a deceased doctor sent the obituary in to the local paper. The doctor's wife brought an action against the mistress claiming the obituary insinuated, first, that the doctor had been unfaithful to his wife and, second, that, in death, the doctor had been finally freed from his wife's influence! Again, however, in this 1995 lawsuit, the living plaintiff, the doctor's wife, was ultimately unsuccessful because the court held that she had not established the three elements required of plaintiffs in libel actions. However, the two lawsuits illustrate the fact that the courts are

"Don't Speak Ill of John Dillinger"

Moving south of the border, it is interesting to note a USA Today article titled "If you're going to fete Dillinger, call this man first."[10] *Apparently Jeff Scalf is a descendent of Dillinger, (his "grandmother was Dillinger's half sister")*[11] *and he has begun several American court actions against parties who have published allegedly false information about Dillinger. Though a criminal, Dillinger was never found guilty of murder and, if it is published that Dillenger was a murderer, Mr. Scalf claims that it is potentially harmful to his own public reputation as one of Dillinger's descendents.*

prepared to consider libel actions based upon obituaries primarily focusing upon deceased persons but, indirectly, potentially having an effect upon the reputations of the living.

There are a number of defences available if you are sued for libel.

1. As stated succinctly in a 1971 case in Manitoba, "What is true cannot be defamatory."[12] You are protected from a claim of defamation if you can prove, on a balance of probabilities, that what you have said is in fact true, even if it injures the reputation of the person about whom it is said. This is known as the defence of justification. (It is not enough that you thought that what you published was true: you must be able to prove it to be true.)

2. A defamation suit against you will also fail if you can show that the plaintiff consented to having the information about him or her published. The person's consent "must be clearly established."[13] Relying on a person's oral consent to go ahead with printing something harmful may not be enough because it will be difficult to prove to the judge or jury involved that you had consent, if the other person later denies the consent and sues you for libel. An audio recording of the consent or a written consent will be helpful in this context.

3. Even if you do not have a person's consent to comment about her or him, and even if what you say cannot be proven to be true, and even if what you have said could potentially be considered defamatory, it will not be held by a court to be defamatory if you are able to establish that the circumstances of its publication bring you within the defence of fair comment. To rely on this defence, you will need to be able to prove that:

a. the statement was an honest expression of your beliefs (in other words, an opinion);

b. your opinion was based upon facts that are true;

c. in making the statement about this individual you were commenting on a matter of public interest; and

d. your statement was not made maliciously.[14]

The first element of the defence of fair comment, the requirement that the statement published be an honest statement of belief by the person who is alleged to have published the libel used to pose a problem where the statement was, indeed, the honest opinion of the author of the piece but it was not necessarily that author who subsequently made the statement public and therefore libelled the plaintiff and the libel was, in turn, not necessarily the honest opinion of those who did publish it and were being sued for libel. Just recently, in the case of *WIC Radio Ltd and Raif Mair v. Simpson*,[15] the Supreme Court has stated that the law of libel must be changed to encompass a wider defence of fair comment because the law of defamation needed to be brought into harmony with the protection of freedom of expression in the *Canadian Charter of Rights and Freedoms*.[16] The Supreme Court's expansion of the defence of fair comment will now provide a potential defence to an editor of a genealogical publication, for example, if the publication includes opinions from contributors that may be otherwise considered libellous but satisfy the requirements of the fair comment defence.

With respect to the fourth element of the defence of fair comment, that if malice is shown to have been a motive behind your comment the defence of fair comment will not succeed, a definition of malice was given by the Supreme Court in its 1995 reasons for decision in *Botiuk v. Toronto Free Press Publications Ltd*.[17] The Court said "malice is commonly understood as ill will toward someone, but it also relates to any indirect motive which conflicts with the sense of duty created by the occasion."[18] Thus, "malice" in the context of a libel lawsuit is more about the situation surrounding the publication than it is about just the state of mind of the person who published the libellous comment.

The defences in a libel lawsuit in Quebec have differed from the defences available elsewhere in Canada. A key concern in Quebec is "whether the publication was in the public interest."[19] If it can be proven that the publication of the statement was in the public interest and that the statement was not published maliciously, the defence of fair comment will succeed in Quebec.

Refer to Crawford, Michael G., The Journalist's Legal Guide, *5th edition (Toronto: Carswell, 2008) for further discussion of differences in defamation law between Quebec and the rest of Canada. The Supreme Court has now added a defence of "responsible communication on matters of public interest" to the common law defences available in the rest of Canada, as discussed at the end of this chapter.*

There are no reported decisions involving defamation suits brought against genealogists in Canada, and, indeed, there have been very few lawsuits reported that deal with situations similar to those that a genealogist is likely to encounter. However, situations where libel could arise in the field of genealogy can be imagined. Civil actions for libel are still heard by juries, whereas otherwise in Canada, juries are only involved in criminal matters.

Internet Libel

When I give talks, I have frequently been asked by genealogists about the Internet and genealogy from the perspective of defamation law. These concerns are timely because, in today's online world, defamatory material published on the Internet is a growing public concern. However, as in other areas of the law, there are no legal decisions from Canadian courts that deal directly with this emerging issue in the context of genealogy. Indeed, the Supreme Court of Canada has not dealt with a case involving defamation in an Internet context, let alone an Internet context involving genealogy. However, the Ontario Court of Appeal, in a case called *Barrick Gold Corporation v. Lopehandia et al.*,[20] has made it clear that Internet postings, because they are globally accessible, can be defamatory. Mr. Lopehandia had posted messages, many times, to many forums and message boards on the Internet, making accusations of false land claims and criminal conduct against Barrick Gold Corporation and its employees by name. Barrick Gold Corporation is headquartered in Ontario but Mr. Lopehandia was in British Columbia when making his postings. Nevertheless, it was held that the Ontario courts had jurisdiction to censure the activities of Mr. Lopehandia (by ordering him to stop such postings in the future and also assessing a monetary penalty against him for having made such postings in the past). Thus, a genealogist, in considering posting material to the Internet, must consider the possible consequences of such a posting from the perspective not only of the jurisdiction in which the genealogist is located but also from the perspective of the myriad jurisdictions in which those who may access the posting will be seated.

The libel cases that have been heard by various Canadian courts, including the *Barrick* case just discussed, make it clear that the courts intend to treat the substance of the law of defamation in similar ways whether the material concerned has been published in a traditional format, such as a paperback, or in digital form through the Internet. In *Barrick*, the courts penalized the defendants for a long series of postings over time; in a recent case in British Columbia (*Manno v. Henry*[21]) the court penalized people involved in a one-time online publishing of one article that defamed a number of people.

Indeed, the context of the Internet may be a little different from the off-line world in the eyes of courts in the sense that, as shown by the Ontario cases of *Warman v. Grosvenor*[22] and *Manson v. Moffett*,[23] courts are prepared to censure online defamatory conduct even if the lawsuit is brought against the person who posted the material a long time after the posting. Mr. Warman, a lawyer with the Government of Canada, successfully sued Mr. Grosvenor over material that Mr. Grosvenor had disseminated over a number of years before the suit was launched via his website, message board postings, and e-mails to Mr. Warman. Thus, if a genealogist posts material to a website or a bulletin board or otherwise disseminates it via the Internet, and that material offends someone else, either within the same jurisdiction or elsewhere, it is possible that such another person could sue the genealogist, in relation to that posting, a good while after the posting was made and the courts will still entertain the lawsuit.

Thus, it is important that you keep in mind, in working with your genealogical research, what you are recording or writing about individuals. Is what you are writing fully supported by reliable sources that you have identified? How widely are you planning to circulate what you are recording or writing? Who may have the chance to read or hear your words? It is important to consider other people's potential reactions to your research when you decide whether or not to release your research to the public in either an off-line or online context. If you look to the principles to which good journalists adhere — thoroughly checking and documenting your facts, writing with an eye to fairly describing your findings, and being sensitive to the fact that the information you have collected can reach others' ears, whether you intend it or not, if you decide to share your findings with even one other person — you should have little concern about being successfully sued with respect to your genealogical research based on allegations of libel.

In its most recent decision, released 22 December 2009, the Supreme Court commented, in a libel case involving an article published in the *Toronto Star* in 2001, that

> many actions now concern blog postings and other online media which are potentially both more ephemeral and more ubiquitous than traditional print media. While established journalistic standards provide a useful guide by which to evaluate the conduct of journalists and non-journalists alike, the applicable standards will necessarily evolve to keep pace with the norms of new communications media.[24]

GLOSSARY

Access to information   In the early 1980s, across Canada, a change in government attitudes led to a series of statutes that legislate access to government-held information for anyone requesting that access — unless there is a legislated reason why the public sector organization from which access is requested must not release the information.

Agency   Agency is a well-developed concept in law. It arises where one person is legally permitted or authorized to act in the place of another; in other situations, the law does not permit a person to act through an agent, but only in person.

Burial plot   Cemeteries in Canada are operated according to various statutes. Customers of the cemeteries typically do not actually buy land within a cemetery. Instead, customers contract for particular rights to a plot of land, including "interment rights" — the right to bury given corpses. The land actually remains in the ownership of the cemetery. In some situations, it is the burial of ashes, rather than corpses, that is permitted.

Consent   Consent is a concept that is relevant to many areas of law and there are many learned treatises about it. In this discussion of genealogy, the concept of consent has arisen in the context of both personal data protection and libel law. One succinct definition is from the *Shorter Oxford English Dictionary*: "Voluntary agreement or acquiescence in what another proposes or desires." If you are relying on another's consent to certain actions, it is best to have written evidence of that consent.

Copyright This area of law is federally regulated in Canada and virtually exclusively governed under the *Copyright Act*. The *Copyright Act*, however, contains three different sets of rights, a large bundle of economic rights, three moral rights, and a collection of exceptions to these rights that Canada's Chief Justice has termed "users' rights." The economic and moral rights attach to literary, artistic, musical, and dramatic expressions of ideas as soon as they are created. Some economic rights attach also to sound recordings, performers' performances, and broadcasts when they are created.

Damages This is the term used when a court orders a defendant in a lawsuit to pay to the successful plaintiff a sum of money set by the court. According to the *Oxford English Dictionary*, the term "damage" in this context was in use as early as 1542 for "the value estimated in money of something lost or withheld; the sum claimed or awarded in compensation for loss or injury sustained."

Fair dealing This is a concept created in Canada's *Copyright Act*. If you do anything with a work (or sound recording, performer's performance, or broadcast) that would otherwise infringe copyright in that work, but you do it fairly, for any one of five purposes, you will not infringe the copyright in that work. The five purposes are (1) research, (2) private study, (3) criticism, (4) review, and (5) news reporting. If your purpose is one of the latter three, you must mention the source with which you are dealing and, if given in the source, the creator. For a use lying within any one of the five purpose categories, the Supreme Court has articulated six factors to consider in deciding whether that use is fair.

Interment rights   Under the *Cemeteries Act* (Ontario), "'interment rights' include the right to require or direct the interment of human remains in a 'lot' and 'interment rights holder' means a person with interment rights with respect to a lot."

Lot   The *Cemeteries Act* (Ontario) defines a "lot" as "an area of land in a cemetery containing, or set aside to contain, human remains and includes a tomb, crypt, or compartment in a mausoleum and a niche or compartment in a columbarium."

Moral rights   The moral rights are a group of rights set out in the *Copyright Act*. Both moral rights and economic rights arise as soon as a work is created. The *Copyright Act* declares that the economic rights will be owned by the employer in an employment situation. The moral rights, on the other hand, always stay with the author or creator. They last just as long as the economic rights — generally the life of the author plus roughly 50 years. The economic rights, however, can be bought, sold, and licensed. The moral rights cannot, although the author can waive them.

Organization   Under public sector personal data protection legislation in Canadian jurisdictions, the organizations to which a statute applies are usually listed as part of the legislation. In the private sector, the federal *Personal Information Protection and Electronic Documents Act* [PIPEDA] applies to all organizations engaged in commercial activities (except where the legislation of a given province applies instead). PIPEDA gives its own broad statutory meaning to the concept of the "organization," including not only incorporated companies but also partnerships and sole proprietorships.

Personal data protection Personal data protection is a legislative concept that arose in the last quarter of the twentieth century, as the ability to gather, use, organize, and store vast amounts of text and recorded data became increasingly possible in the computer age. The original notion of guidelines for organizations to follow in the "cradle to grave" management of information about individuals arose out of a concern to balance privacy interests with ensuring the portability of data. Personal data protection legislation may be distinguished from privacy law, in part, because personal data protection legislation does not give organizations any ability to gather information from individuals (*whether* to gather information from individuals) but, rather, accepting that an organization has decided to gather such data, or is otherwise mandated to do so, legislates *how* that gathering shall be done and what the further treatment of the data, in the hands of the organization, will be.

Personal information "Personal information" is generally a defined term in the various codifications of personal data protection in the provinces, territories, and federal jurisdiction in Canada. Each particular statute should be checked as need arises. Generally, though, the term is used to refer to data about an individual that is clearly linked to that individual. Absent a particular exception to the contrary in a statute, such information will be protected by statute from being released, by a public body or a private sector business, to anyone other than the individual who is the subject of it. However, the statutes do sometimes declare that information that would otherwise appear to be personal information will not be treated as such under the statute. For example, under PIPEDA, "'personal information' does *not* include the name, title, or business address or telephone number of any employee of an organization." [emphasis added]

Privacy Privacy is perhaps most succinctly described as the state of being let alone. A person can keep private information on all manner of subjects, not just personal information. In Canada, privacy is not nearly so well or universally protected in law across the country as is personal data. The province with the most comprehensive protection for privacy is Quebec.

Private In personal data protection law, it is important to distinguish public sector organizations, which are almost universally subject to both access legislation and personal data protection legislation, from private sector organizations, which, if they are engaged in commercial activities, are governed by personal data protection legislation but not by any access legislation.

Public Public has many meanings in law. In this discussion of genealogy it has occurred in connection with the public sector institutions that are named under the various provincial, territorial, and federal statutes as being required to adhere to each personal data protection statute and access legislation. It has also been used in connection with the exclusive Canadian monopoly of the copyright holder to communicate a "work to the public by telecommunication." It has been discussed in terms of the attitudes of the various provinces and territories toward public access as expressed in their statutes governing cemeteries. Finally, it has been discussed in terms of publishing libellous statements and the consequences thereof. Each meaning of "public" has been specific to the context of the area of law in which it is discussed.

Record The "record" is a concept used in most personal data protection regimes in Canada and is generally widely defined to include text artifacts such as correspondence, books, e-mails, and so on, as well as pictures, videos, sound recordings, and so on. It includes computerized records. Upon request, organizations are required to produce all the records relevant to a request. These records are then screened to see whether, under the applicable statute, the requestor is entitled to all or parts of each of them.

Work The "work" is the fundamental concept in copyright law. Works can be any one of four types: literary, artistic, musical, or dramatic. The *Copyright Act* also gives a creator a more limited set of rights over "other subject matter" — that is, over sound recordings, broadcasts, and performers' performances. These latter are typically not materials that would involve a genealogist — although it may be worth noting that any recording of an interview (such as an oral history recording) will involve considering the rights of the person who made the recording.

STATUTES CITED

Chapters 1 and 2
(Other than those listed on pages 17–18 and 23–24)

Alberta: *Personal Information Protection Act*, S.A. 2003, c. P-6.5

British Columbia: *Personal Information Protection Act*, S.B.C. 2003, c. 63

British Columbia: *Privacy Act*, R.S.B.C. 1996, c. 372

Canada: *Access to Information Act*, R.S.C. 1985, c. A-1

Canada: *An Act to Amend the Statistics Act*, S.C. 2005, c. 31

Canada: *Copyright Act*, R.S.C. 1985, c. C-42

Canada: *Canadian Human Rights Act*, [1977] 25-26 Eliz.II, c. 33, Pt.IV, ss. 49-62

Canada: *Personal Information Protection and Electronic Documents Act*, S.C. 2000, c. 5

Canada: *Privacy Act*, R.S.C. 1985, c. P-21

Manitoba: *Privacy Act*, R.S.M. 1987, c. P125

Newfoundland and Labrador: *Privacy Act*, R.S.N.L. 1990, c. P-22

Ontario: *Access to Adoption Records Act (Vital Statistics Statute Law Amendment), 2008*, S.O. 2008, c. 5

Ontario: *Public Sector Salary Disclosure Act, 1996*, S.O.1996, c.1, Schedule A

Quebec: *Act Respecting the Protection of Personal Information in the Private Sector*, R.S.Q. c. P-39.1

Quebec: *Charter of Rights and Freedoms*, R.S.Q. c. C-12

Quebec: *Civil Code of Quebec*, S.Q. 1991, c. 64

Saskatchewan: *Privacy Act*, R.S.S. 1978, c. P-24

Chapter 3

Canada: *Copyright Act*, R.S.C. 1985, c. C-42

Canada: *Personal Information Protection and Electronic Documents Act*, S.C. 2000, c. 5

Ontario: *Municipal Freedom of Information and Protection of Privacy Act in Ontario*, R.S.O. 1990, c. M

Chapter 4

Canada: *Copyright Act*, R.S.C. 1985, c. C-42

Canada: *Libraries and Archives of Canada Act*, S.C. 2004, c. 11

Chapter 5

Canada: *Charter of Rights and Freedoms*

CASED REFERRED TO

Chapters 1 and 2

Thames Valley District School Board, Ontario Information and Privacy Commissioner Order MO-2467, 27 October 2009 (Adjudicator Bhattacharjee).

Chapter 3

Kilvington Brothers Ltd. v. Goldberg, (1957), 8 D.L.R. (2d) 768 (OntSupCt) Judson J.

Toronto Economic Development Corporation v. Ontario (Information and Privacy Commissioner), an unreported decision of the Ontario Divisional Court from 14 November 2006.

Chapter 4

CCH Ltd. v. Law Society of Upper Canada [2004] 1 S.C.R. 339 (SCC) McLachlin C.J.

Society of Composers, Authors and Music Publishers of Canada [SOCAN] v. Canadian Association of Internet Providers, [2004] S.C.J. No. 44 (SCC) McLachlin, C.J.

Chapter 5

Allen v. Bailey [1995] O.J. 974 (OntCtGD) Kennedy, J.

Barnes v. Carter [1910] O.J .309 (OntCtHJ) Middleton, J.

Barrick Gold Corporation v. Lopehandia et al. (2001) 71 O.R. (3d) 416 (OCA) per Blair, J.A.

Botiuk v. Toronto Free Press Publications Ltd. [1995] 3 S.C.R. 3 (SCC) Cory, J.

Cherneskey v. Armadale Publishers Ltd. [1979] 1 S.C.R. 1067 (SCC) Laskin, C.J.

Chiniquy v. Begin (1915), 24 D.L.R. 687 (QueQB) Archambeault, C.J.

Courchene v. Marlborough Hotel Co. (1971) 20 D.L.R (3d) 109 (ManQB) Tritschler, C.J.Q.B.

Grant v. Torstar Corp., 2009 SCC 61.

Hodgson v. Canadian Newspapers Co. [1998], 39 O.R. (3d) 235 (OnCtGD) Lane, J.

Manno v. Henry [2008] B.C.J. No. 1057 (BCSC), J.C. Grauer, J.

Manson v. Moffett [2008] O.J. No. 1697 (OSC), K.A. Hoilett, J.

Syms v. Warren (1976), 71 D.L.R. (3d) 558 (ManQB) Hamilton, J.

Warman v. Grosvenor [2008] O.J. No. 4462 (OSC), L.C. Rathusny, J.

WIC Radio Ltd and Raif Mair v. Simpson (2008), 293 D.L.R. (4th) 513 (SCC) Binnie, J.

NOTES

Chapter 1

1. See Barbara Turner Kinsella, "Loss Doesn't Go Away," *Toronto Star*, 27 September 2008; available at *pqasb.pqarchiver.com/ thestar/access/1562490911.html?dids=1562490911:1562490 911&FMT=ABS&FMTS=ABS:FT&type=current&date=Sep +27,=2008&author=Barbara+Turner+Kinsella&pub=Toronto +Star&edition=&startpage=L.1&desc='Loss+doesn't+go+away' ;+Search+for+missing+father+spans+21+years.+Finally,+this+ month,+a+daughter+finds+answers.*

2. New Brunswick's *Right to Information Act*, SNB 1978, c. R-10.3, gives a right of access to "information relating to the public business of the Province" (s. 2).

3. Colin H.H. McNairn and Christopher D. Woodbury, *Government Information:Access and Privacy* (Carswell, updated to 2008), 3–2. New Brunswick's *Protection of Personal Information Act* incorporates, in s. 2(2), a "Statutory Code of Practice," Schedule A to the Act that, in turn, provides as "Principle 3: Consent" that "The consent of the individual is required for the collection, use, or disclosure of personal information,

except where inappropriate."

4. Quebec. *An Act Respecting Access to Documents Held By Public Bodies and the Protection of Personal Information*, s. 68(2).

5. See "Fifth Census of Canada, 1911: Instructions to Officers, Commissioners and Enumerators" (Approved by Order in Council 31 March 1911), paragraph 23.

6. In the case of *Beatty v. Canada (Attorney General)* [2005] 1 F.C.R. 327, Justice Gibson did not give the applicant, "an amateur family historian," the orders that she sought which would have given her access to individual returns for the 1911 Census through the National Archives, saying:

> [b]ecause the tension between the protection of privacy and access to information held by the Government of Canada for the purposes of research is a policy question, and as Parliament clearly indicated its intention to reserve to the Governor in Council and, eventually to itself, the resolution of issues arising out of that tension, the Court concluded that it had to be very cautious and declined to intervene on the facts of this matter....

7. See *An Act to Amend the Statistics Act*, s. 1 (which became law 29 June 2005), specifically with respect to its amendment of the *Statistics Act*, R.S.C. 1985, c. S-19, by adding s. 18.1(2):

> The information contained in the returns of each census of the population taken in 2006 or later is no longer subject to [the secrecy provisions of the Act] ninety-two years after the census is taken, but only if the person to whom the information relates

consents, at the time of the census, to the release of the information ninety-two years later.

8. Canada. *An Act to Amend the Statistics Act*, s. 1, amending the *Statistics Act* by adding s. 18.1(1):

> The information contained in the returns of each census of population taken between 1910 and 2005 is no longer subject to [the secrecy provisions of the Act] ninety-two years after the census is taken.

9. See s. 2 of the *Act to Amend the Statistics Act*, which mandates a review of the new section giving individual control to release after 92 years to the individuals responding to the census and otherwise permanently prohibiting the release of the individual information.

10. The Library of Parliament published a Legislative Summary of Bill S-18, the bill that eventually became the *Act to Amend the Statistics Act*, prepared by James R. Robertson (Principal) and Benjamin R. Dolin. This brief document outlines the history of this issue and the tension between access and privacy in the twentieth-century census records, including a number of committees, reports, and other bills that had failed. It is because of the failure of the other bills that I predict that the compromise created by Bill S-18, which does not provide full access, will continue, even after the mandated review some years in the future.

11. Motokoff, Gary, "These Are the Times that Try Men's Souls," in *Nu? What's New?: The E-zine of Jewish Genealogy From Avotaynu*, Vol. 10, No. 8, 26 April 2009; available at: *www.avotaynu.com/nu/V10N08.htm*.

12. *Thames Valle District School Board*, Ontario Information and Privacy Commissioner Order MO-2467, 27 October 2009 (Adjudicator Bhattacharjee).
13. s. 4(2)(b).

Chapter 2

1. s. 1.
2. s. 4(2).
3. s. 2.
4. s. 4(2).
5. s. 2.
6. Schedule 1, s. 4.3 of PIPEDA.
7. s. 7(1)(d).
8. Miner, John, "Man Searching for Sperm Donor Dad," *The London Free Press*, 26 June 2009, A3.
9. s. 7(1)(d).
10. s. 11(1).
11. s. 11(2).

Chapter 3

1. *Families* 41(1), 15–18.
2. *www.rcec.london.on.ca/08/contact09.html*.
3. Cemeteries that are part of municipalities include, for example, such cemeteries as Park Cemetery (owned by the Township of Lanark Highlands); Bexley, Burnt River, Coboconk, Graham, Kinmount, Lakeside South Valentia, Lake Dalrymple, Lake View, Mud Lake, Pine Grove, and Woodville Knox Presbyterian (all owned by the City of

Kawartha Lakes); Greenwood and Fairview (owned by the Township of Halton Hills); and Groveside (owned by the Township of Whitby).

4. *www.niagarafalls.ca/city_hall/departments/parks_recreation_and_ culture/cemetery/index.asp*; accessed 5 August 2009.

5. I am indebted to members of the various Branches of the Ontario Genealogical Society who made me aware that there were municipal cemeteries: I had not encountered them prior to meeting members of the Society and discussing them with them.

6. *The Cemeteries Act*, s. 1.

7. s. 50(2).

8. s. 50(3).

9. s. 50(5).

10. s. 113(2)4. iii.

11. s. 113(2)4. iv.

12. s. 50(6).

13. See *www.gov.on.ca/ont/portal/!ut/p/.cmd/cs/.ce/7_0_A/.s/7_ 0252/_s.7_0_A/7_0_252/_1/en?docid=004.*

14. Mount Pleasant Cemetery Bylaws online, section 1.1, see *www. mountpleasantgroupofcemeteries.ca/our_cemeteries/Cemetery%20 By-laws.pdf.*

15. *www.nbrcc.ca/admin.htm.*

16. North Bay Catholic Cemeteries Bylaw 6.5.

17. Mount Pleasant Group of Cemeteries Bylaw 1.2.

18. North Bay Catholic Cemeteries Bylaw 6.7 and Mount Pleasant Group of Cemeteries Bylaw 1.2.

19. This information came to me from questions and examples given by audience members at a number of presentations I made to area genealogy meetings in Ontario in 2005–06.

20. *Cemeteries Act*, Statutes of Saskatchewan, 1999, c.c-4.01, as amended, s.53(2).

21. Statutes of British Columbia 2004, c.35.

22. *Cemeteries Act*, Revised Statutes of Alberta 2000, c. c-3; *Cemeteries Act*, Continuing Consolidation of the Statutes of Manitoba, c. c30; *Cemetery Companies Act*, Revised Statutes of New Brunswick 1973, c. c-1; *Cemetery Companies Act*, Revised Statutes of Nova Scotia 1989.c. 63; *Cemeteries Act*, Revised Statutes of Prince Edward Island 1988, c. c-2.

23. *www.niagarafalls.ca/city_hall/departments/parks_recreation_and_culture/cemetery/index.asp.*

24. Regulation 130/92.

25. s. 2.

26. Revised Statutes of Ontario, c. M-56.

27. MFIPPA, s.2, and Ontario Regulation 372/91, as amended by Reg. 420/04.

28. *Toronto Economic Development Corporation v. Ontario* (Information and Privacy Commissioner), an unreported decision of the Ontario Divisional Court from 14 November 2006.

29. MFIPPA, s. 2(2).

30. PIPEDA, s.7(3)(h).

31. PIPEDA, s. 7(3)(i).

32. *Copyright Act*, Revised Statutes of Canada 1985, c. C-42, s. 5.

33. *Copyright Act*, s. 6.

34. 8 Dominion Law Reports (2d) 768 (Supreme Court of Ontario).

35. *Copyright Act*, s. 3.

36. *Copyright Act*, s. 3.

37. *Copyright Act*, s. 29.

38. For further information about the interpretation of fair dealing and users' rights under the *Copyright Act*, please see Margaret Ann Wilkinson, "Filtering the Flow from the Fountains of Knowledge: Access and Copyright in Education

and Libraries," in Michael Geist (ed.) *In the Public Interest: The Future of Canadian Copyright Law* (Toronto: Irwin Law, 2005), 331–74. Also available online at *www.irwinlaw.com/pages/content-commons/filtering-the-flow-from-the-fountains-of-knowledge--access-and-copyright-in-education-and-libraries--margaret-anne-wilkinson.*

39. *www.archives.gov.on.ca/english/archivalrecorecords/interloan/cemetery.aspx*; accessed 4 August 2009.

Chapter 4

1. See, for example, *Allen v. Bailey* [1995] O.J. 974.
2. This is language used by the Supreme Court of Canada in *CCH Ltd. v. Law Society of Upper Canada*, decided in 2004.
3. See the judgment of the Supreme Court in *CCH Ltd. v. Law Society of Upper Canada.*
4. See s. 32.1 of the *Copyright Act.*
5. The Supreme Court of Canada wrote about this in 2004, in its decision in the case known as "Tariff 22," properly styled *Society of Composers, Authors and Music Publishers of Canada [SOCAN] v. Canadian Association of Internet Providers.*
6. See the *Copyright Act*, s. 13(2).
7. See the Copyright Board of Canada website, *www.cb-cda.gc.ca.*
8. *Copyright Act*, s. 14.
9. *Copyright Act*, s. 77. The website of the Copyright Board provides full information on this process.
10. Under the Canadian *Patent Act.*
11. See s. 10(2)(d) of the *Library and Archives of Canada Act, 2004* and the *Legal Deposit of Publications Regulations* [the *Regulations*], SOR/2006-337, s. 4 (which came into force on 1 January 2007).

12. See s. 4(b) of the Regulations.
13. See sections 4(a) and 4(l), respectively, of the Regulations.
14. Section 4(p) of the Regulations.

Chapter 5

1. Brown, Raymond E., *Defamation Law: A Primer* (Toronto: Carswell, 2003), 26.
2. (Toronto: Emond Montgomery Publications, 2006), 269.
3. Crawford, Michael G., *The Journalist's Legal Guide,* 5th Edition (Toronto: Carswell, 2008), 68.
4. In Canada, it is possible that libel will be prosecuted under the *Criminal Code* but this situation is rare and will not be dealt with in this discussion.
5. [1979] 1 S.C.R. 1067.
6. *Trustee Act* R.S.O. 1990, Chapter T.23, s. 38(1).
7. [1910] O.J. 309 (OntHC).
8. *Chiniquy v. Begin* (1915), 24 D.L.R. 687 (QueCA).
9. [1995] O.J. No 974 (OntCtGD).
10. Keen, Judy. "If You're Going to Fete Dillinger, Call This Man First." *USA Today*, March 6, 2007; accessed 22 May 2009; available at *www.usatoday.com/news/nation/2007-06-03-dillinger_N.htm.*
11. *Ibid.*
12. *Courchene v. Marlborough Hotel Co.* (1971) 20 D.L.R. (3d) 109 (ManQB), paragraph 11.
13. *Syms v. Warren* (1976), 71 D.L.R. (3d) 558 (ManQB).
14. Brown, supra, 171.
15. [2008], 293 D.L.R. (4th) 513 (SCC).
16. *Ibid.*, at para 2. Ontario's *Libel and Slander Act*, s.24, for example, already had broadened the common law defence

of fair comment to allow the defence as long as the person *could* "honestly hold the opinion," regardless if they actually *did* hold it.

17. [1995] 3 S.C.R. 3.

18. *Ibid.*, paragraph 79.

19. *WIC Radio Ltd and Raif Mair v. Simpson*, cited supra, note 15.

20. [2001] 71 O.R. (3d) 416 (Ontario Court of Appeal) per Blair, J.A.

21. [2008] B.C.J. No. 1057 (BCSC), Grauer, J.

22. [2008] O.J. No. 4462 (OntSC), Rathusny, J.

23. [2008] O.J. No.1697 (OntSC), Hoilett, J.

24. *Grant v. Torstar Corp.* 2009 SCC 61 para 97, per McLachlin, C.J., for the majority.

OTHER GENEALOGIST'S

REFERENCE SHELF TITLES

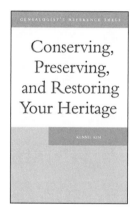

**CONSERVING, PRESERVING,
AND RESTORING YOUR HERITAGE**
A Professional's Advice
Kennis Kim
978-1-55488-462-9 $19.99

Our family history may be held in documents, photographs, books, clothing, or textiles; sometimes complete collections of items such as coins, trading cards, or stamps. As custodians of pieces of our history, we are faced with how to maintain these items. Here's all you need to determine what you can do yourself to preserve your precious things for future generations.

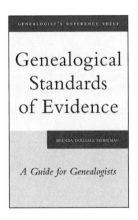

GENEALOGICAL STANDARDS OF EVIDENCE
A Guide for Family Historians
Brenda Dougall Merriman
978-1-55488-451-3 $19.99

Genealogy and family history revolve around issues of identification. Genealogical evidence is the information — analyzed and evaluated — that allows us to identify an individual and event in his or her life, or the relationship between individuals. This book will tell you about how the genealogical community developed standards of evidence and documentation, what those standards are, and how you can apply them to your own work.

PUBLISH YOUR FAMILY HISTORY
Preserving Your Heritage in a Book
Susan Yates and Greg Ioannou
978-1-55488-727-9 $19.99

Many people want to write a family history, but few ever take on the job of publishing one. *Publish Your Family History* will tell you all the fundamentals of book production, together with the important details that distinguish a home-published book from a homemade one.

Available at your favourite bookseller.

DUNDURN
www.dundurn.com